MW00773322

STANDOUT
STARTUP

STANDOUT STARTUP

THE FOUNDER'S GUIDE TO
IRRESISTIBLE
MARKETING
THAT FUELS GROWTH

ALLYSON LETTERI

COSTA FLORA

Copyright © 2023 by Allyson Letteri

All rights reserved. No part of this book may be reproduced or transmitted in any form or by any means, electronic or mechanical, including photocopying, recording, or any other information storage and retrieval system, without prior permission in writing from the publisher or author.

This publication is designed to provide accurate and authoritative information in regard to the subject matter covered. While the publisher and author have used their best efforts in preparing this book, they make no representations or warranties with respect to the accuracy or completeness of the contents of this book. No responsibility for loss or damage occasion to any person, acting, or refraining from action, as a result of the material in this publication can be accepted by the publisher or the author.

The story, all names, characters, and incidents portrayed in this production are fictitious. Only the companies that are mentioned by name, which are the author's past employers, are real companies. No identification with actual persons (living or deceased), places, buildings, and products is intended or should be inferred.

Published by Costa Flora
Edited by Olivia Peluso
Cover designed by Vanessa Mendozzi
Interior designed by Sheer Design and Typesetting

ISBN 979-8-9888392-9-3 (e-book)
ISBN 979-8-9888392-2-4 (paperback)

1st edition September 2023

Visit the author's website at allysonletteri.com

To Vini, Beckett, and Isla.
Thank you for filling my life with joy, adventure, and love.

BONUS

STANDOUT STARTUP TOOLKIT

This book is filled with step-by-step guidance and useful templates so you can create an effective messaging and content strategy. Download a free toolkit with the templates and worksheets from *Standout Startup*, ready for you to complete. It's the fastest way to take action and get results.

allysonletteri.com/toolkit

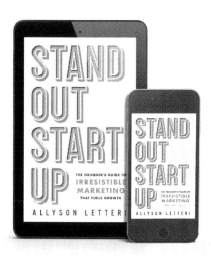

CONTENTS

PART 3:

CREATE A CONTENT STRATEGY THAT DRIVES GROWTH

MESSAGING IS AN ESSENTIAL FOUNDER SKILL SET

You've launched an innovative product that will change your customers' lives for the better. But now you need great product messaging. Without it, getting traction with customers is going to be slow—or even impossible.

You probably already know this. I've worked with many tech startup founders who, after we start to dig into their marketing strategy and goals, say it's a challenge to get their ideal customers interested in their product. They need to know how to make their startup's product stand out to unlock user growth.

Effective product messaging is the backbone of a successful marketing strategy. No matter how well your product delivers results, if you can't explain who it's for, what it does, and why it's better than the alternatives, you won't attract and retain customers.

"I'm losing potential customers every day because our messaging is wrong," the cofounder of a Series A climate tech startup told me in frustration. "My business development team doesn't know how to explain the value of our product. Their pitch is all wrong, and I'm overwhelmed trying to fix it." Her company's growth had stalled, and the team needed a way to explain to prospects why their product was a better choice than legacy solutions.

Another founder winced as he shared, "Our target audience just doesn't get it." His seed stage fintech startup was struggling to grow app downloads. "Our product is so clearly superior to everything else on the market. But something about how we're describing the app just isn't connecting. Choosing us should be a no-brainer for people who want the best financial returns, but they're not signing up."

Other times, leaders tell me their messaging can't keep pace with their product updates. In the early days leading up to launch, their startup created a website, developed emails, and built a sales deck. But this collateral quickly became outdated as their product changed. Their marketing messages no longer explain the value of their ever-improving product. The result? Customer conversion plateaus—or tanks.

In other cases, opportunity knocks, and a startup has the chance to expand into a new customer segment. The founder knows that their product can appeal to a broader or different audience. But the startup needs to reposition what they're selling to grow beyond its niche. They need updated value propositions to attract a new set of customers. Oftentimes the team gets stuck when trying to find the right way to describe their product to this unique customer segment.

It's no surprise that when founders sense that their messaging is weak, they feel like the rest of their marketing is confusing or chaotic. They also don't know what content to create, because they're not sure what their ideal customers need to know to buy and engage with their product. Founders can feel paralyzed, especially if they don't have a marketing team yet to figure all of this out.

But here's the good news: There's a clear process you can use to get unstuck, create powerful product messaging, and develop content that drives growth. And it doesn't require you to be a marketer. That's exactly what you'll learn how to do with this book. This guide reveals how to make your startup standout and use marketing to engage your ideal customers.

WHY DO YOU NEED POWERFUL PRODUCT MESSAGING?

During my 15 years working as a marketing leader at high-growth Silicon Valley startups, I led teams to develop and launch effective go-to-market strategies. In each of these companies, a central part of our work was creating effective product messaging and then high-converting content for every step of the customer journey. I now work as a marketing advisor to early stage tech startup leaders, and refreshing these startups' messaging is almost always a pivotal part of our work. After that, we can develop a much more effective (and efficient) content and growth marketing strategy.

As a startup founder, you're the company's first product marketer. You're the one creating the messaging for your initial website, new sales process, and early investor pitches. You're constantly on the hook to explain what's so great about your product and how it's unique so that you can close sales and get funding.

It's helpful that the customer insights you need to guide a product roadmap, acquire initial customers, and find product-market fit (PMF) overlap with the information you need to define effective messaging. These are interrelated, high-stakes processes for a startup. The work that goes into developing personas, positioning, brand personality, and messaging (all of which you'll learn how to do in this book) is so core to a startup's product and growth strategy that it's a miss to consider it simply "marketing" work. It's some of the most strategic work a startup founder and their team can do to get traction.

Effective product messaging converts prospects and engages customers. It helps your startup:

✦ **Attract the right customers:** Your ideal customers will quickly recognize that your product is for them, that it can solve a problem they're facing, and that it's better than the alternative solutions out there.

✦ **Increase sales:** The right messaging demonstrates how your product delivers the exact results your persona is looking for and motivates them to take the next step to sign up or buy.

✦ **Improve retention:** Great messaging ensures customers understand how your product works, actively use key features, and get the results they expect. This increases customer retention.

✦ **Unlock content strategy:** You'll adapt key messages to content for each stage of the customer journey, so your ideal customer connects with your product, has information to make decisions, and takes action in each stage.

✦ **Align your team:** Your entire team will be equipped with your most compelling messages for their own initiatives so your customer touch points will become more cohesive and optimized to convert.

✦ **Build strategic confidence:** With clarity on your ideal customer, positioning, messaging, and content strategy, you'll have greater confidence that you can effectively attract, convert, and retain customers.

Great product messaging will accelerate your company's growth because it helps you reach the right people, effectively convert them into customers, and deliver the results you promised. Knowing how to create this messaging is an incredibly useful skill set to master for any founder, as well as anyone in marketing, sales, or product development. Through the process you follow in this book, you'll foster team alignment, accelerate user growth, increase retention, and improve customer satisfaction. This ultimately leads to revenue growth, too.

HOW TO CREATE POWERFUL PRODUCT MESSAGING

What does it take to create powerful product messaging? I'll guide you through the steps to capture insights about your ideal customers, your competitors, and your category. Then, you'll create a product messaging framework, which will unlock your ability to create an effective content strategy and channel plans. Together, these elements comprise a large part of your go-to-market strategy, which enables you to launch and grow your business with a specific group of customers.

Standout Startup is divided into three parts. First, you'll define your 3 Ps—persona, positioning, and personality—to develop the insights you need to create effective messaging. In part 2, you'll use the 3 Ps to create a strong product messaging framework that includes a unique selling proposition, value propositions, and proof points. Then in part 3, you'll create a content strategy that drives conversion and growth at each stage of the customer journey.

As we move through the book, I'll share step-by-step guidance and templates you can use to complete each part of the process. You'll walk away clear on your positioning and confident about your brand personality. You'll be ready to refresh your website, emails, and sales script with high-converting messaging. And to pull it all together, you'll have a content engine that fuels each of your key channels and offers customers exactly what they need to choose and use your product. **This book is your marketing accelerator.**

One last thing before we dive in: To show you how all of the pieces fit together, here's an overview of what you'll learn in each chapter. You'll also find recommendations at the end of each chapter, called "Standout Strategies," that capture your must-know next steps.

PART 1:
DEFINE YOUR 3 PS TO UNLOCK MESSAGING

1. **Identify your 3 Ps.** Learn the importance of the 3 Ps— persona, positioning, and personality—and why they're essential to creating effective messaging. Find out when you'll need to refresh your 3 Ps and messaging as your product, customers, and competitors evolve.

2. **Decide who you're talking to.** Identify your ideal customer, who's the person that you want to motivate and influence with your messaging. You'll create a persona of this customer, which becomes the filter for all of your messaging decisions. If you sell products to businesses, you'll first create an ideal customer profile (ICP) for the companies that are the best fit for your product, *then* you'll identify your buying committee and create personas.

3. **Capture your persona.** Build a persona with insights that enable you to create powerful messaging. You'll capture your ideal customer's pains, gains, shifts, motivators, and

blockers. These factors help you understand what your ideal customer values so you can create messages that resonate and build trust.

4. **Understand the competition.** Create a shortlist of the other solutions your persona considers when deciding how to solve their pain points. You'll create a competitive map and identify each product's differentiators. Then you'll summarize what makes each of these solutions a desirable choice while also identifying what makes your product superior.

5. **Fill in gaps with research.** Conduct research to develop the additional insights you need to complete your personas and competitive map. Learn a range of effective research techniques you can use to gain the empathy needed to create strong product positioning.

6. **Define your positioning.** Determine the best way to position your product so that customers understand why it's different and better than the range of alternative solutions. Decide how you need to shift perceptions about your product so your persona recognizes that it's the best fit for their needs. Finally, capture your positioning in a unique selling proposition (USP).

7. **Create your personality.** Define a brand character that is unique and appealing to your ideal audience, which will also make your product stand out. Run a workshop filled with brand discovery exercises to define your brand attributes. Then create a tone of voice that enables you to build affinity and communicate consistently with your persona.

PART 2:
DEVELOP POWERFUL PRODUCT MESSAGING

8. **Develop strong value propositions.** Create value propositions that describe the most compelling benefits your product offers. Learn the criteria for effective value propositions that highlight the results your product delivers and entice your persona to buy.

9. **Support with proof points.** Validate your value propositions with proof points that build trust and desire. Learn the types of proof points that establish the most credibility with your ideal customer, and determine what customer stories and information will motivate them to select your product.

10. **Test your messages.** Get customer feedback on your USP, value props, and proof points before you finalize your messaging. Learn effective ways to do research that will help you refine your messages. Then run tests to see what messages drive the highest engagement and conversion with your ideal customers.

11. **Develop your product narrative.** Use your product messaging framework to develop a powerful story that converts customers on your website and in your sales pitch. Create a narrative that will hook your ideal customers, demonstrate the results your product delivers, highlight your differentiators, and share a clear call to action.

12. **Refine your company messages.** Revisit your company's vision, mission, and values, and align them with your updated 3 Ps and product messaging. Make tweaks to

better express your startup's greater purpose in the world and its promise to your ideal customers.

13. **Build your project plan and team.** Find out how to plan and execute this messaging work in six two-week-long sprints. Learn the templates and activities to complete in each sprint so your team can develop, test, and refine your product messaging in just one quarter. Determine the right people to tap on your team to lead and participate in this work.

PART 3:
CREATE A CONTENT STRATEGY THAT DRIVES GROWTH

14. **Prioritize content to fuel the customer journey.** Learn about the five phases of the customer journey and the content your ideal customers need in each phase. Then prioritize your top marketing goals and decide what types of content to create to motivate your customers and achieve these results.

15. **Create your core content plan.** Learn an efficient process to create and launch core content each month to execute your marketing strategy. Find out the value of creating fewer, intentional pieces of content that fuel multiple channels. Then see how to identify timely and relevant content themes that engage your persona.

16. **Choose engaging topics and hooks.** Create irresistible hooks and topics for your content that will catch the attention of and engage your ideal customers. Learn a strategic framework for crafting captivating hooks so you have plenty of options as you adapt content to each channel.

17. **Optimize your owned channel experience.** Create a strong "nurture" and "convert" experience in your owned channels as you roll out your new messaging and content. Learn ways to adapt your core content to create a strong conversion experience.

18. **Fuel acquisition with core content.** Build an effective "attract" strategy to reach your ideal customers through earned, social, and paid channels. Find out how to repurpose your core content to fuel a wide range of acquisition channels.

19. **Drive retention with customer marketing.** Create content for the "onboard" and "engage" phases of your customer journey that encourages customers to actively use your product. Learn the types of content and campaigns that can help your customers get results and become loyal users, driving customer retention and referrals.

20. **Celebrate your growth.** Cheers! You've created major changes in your business that will fuel sustainable customer growth. Revisit the main updates you'll make to your messaging and content strategy. Recognize that by creating a better customer experience, you'll accelerate growth, too. Celebrate with your team and track your success.

In short, this book gives you the tools and guidance you need to make your startup stand out. I wrote *Standout Startup* to speed up success for startup founders and teams who work tirelessly to scale world-changing products. My goal is to make it easier for you to impact the lives of customers who need you the most. You'll start by defining your 3 Ps, so flip to chapter 1 to begin.

PART 1

DEFINE YOUR 3 PS TO UNLOCK MESSAGING

IDENTIFY YOUR 3 PS

The right messaging has the power to convert customers. Product messaging is the way you describe the value and differentiators of your product. Effective messaging catches the attention of your ideal customers and explains why your product is the best option to solve their challenges. It creates a desire for the results that your product delivers. As you build credibility and affinity with your ideal customers, they move closer to buying and using your product.

Developing strong product messaging (and a successful marketing strategy) begins with defining your company's 3 Ps. You'll need to answer these questions:

✦ **Persona:** Who is your ideal customer? What are their needs and desired outcomes from your product?

✦ **Positioning:** Why is your product different and better than the competitors' solutions?

✦ **Personality:** How do you communicate with your persona in an appealing way?

Personas unlock how you communicate the *value* of your product. Your persona's needs, desires, and motivators help you understand the outcomes they seek and what attracts them to different solutions. Knowing this enables you to describe the benefits of your product and the results it delivers in a way that's highly valuable to your ideal customers.

Positioning unlocks how you communicate your product's *differentiators*. First, you need to identify what other products and solutions your persona considers to solve their pain points. Then you need to know why they select these solutions. With this information, you can figure out what will make your product stand out as your persona's best option. You'll capture what makes your product different and better than the alternatives in your product positioning.

Personality unlocks how you build *affinity* with your ideal customers through your brand identity and a consistent communication style. Your brand attributes and the tone of voice you use in your content need to build connection and trust with your audience. A clear, unique personality also helps differentiate your product from the other brands in your space.

Throughout this book, I'll share a range of examples of startups using the 3 Ps to develop their messaging strategy. These companies are mashups, inspired and informed by my real-world experiences working with founders and their teams. You'll meet a handful of these founders and learn their stories soon, including:

✦ Sophia, who builds an ICP and personas for her e-commerce security platform (chapters 2 and 3)

✦ Lucas, who creates a competitive map and content for his freelance recruiter marketplace (chapters 4 and 14)

✦ Caroline, who develops research and a product narrative for her accounting software (chapters 5 and 11)

+ Andrew, who positions his healthcare startup to stand out vs. traditional solutions (chapter 6)

+ Several founders who develop their brand personality to build affinity with customers (chapter 7)

+ William, who tests product messaging for his catering marketplace (chapter 10)

In each example, you'll learn what opportunities these founders faced and the steps they took to create strong messaging.

KNOW WHEN TO UPDATE YOUR MESSAGING

When does your startup need to update its 3 Ps and messaging? You'll need to refresh (or overhaul) your product messaging multiple times as your startup grows. The more interactions you have with your ideal customers, and the more you learn about your competitors, you'll discover the most effective ways to describe your product. Then as your customers, competitors, and product change, you'll need to evolve the way you explain your product's value and differentiators. Your startup will likely need to go through the messaging development process when:

You're trying to find product-market fit (PMF). Even before you know exactly who your ideal customers are and the top competitors you're up against, you'll need to create initial product messaging. The steps in this book will help you develop a strong hypothesis about the customers you're trying to attract, and then craft effective messaging to acquire those initial customers. You'll refine this messaging as you learn more about your exact persona and what makes them choose your product over alternative solutions.

You've identified product-market fit. After launching and iterating on your product to find PMF, you'll have a strong understanding of your ideal customer and competitive advantage. This is the perfect time to codify your learnings into the 3 Ps and update your messaging framework. Then you'll refresh your marketing touchpoints to reflect this new messaging. Synthesizing these insights will help align your entire team on the best messages as you shift into growth mode.

Your messaging is weak or outdated. As one founder shared with me, "I know that our website and sales deck don't represent the best way to talk about our product anymore. It kills me. But there's so much that we need to change; I actually don't know where to start." When your messaging lags behind your product's capabilities or your marketing touchpoints say different things, you need to refresh your messaging. Don't let this persist. Follow the process in this book to update your messages and all of your important collateral.

You want to sell to a new customer segment. As you expand into new customer segments or broaden from an initial niche market, you'll add to your 3 Ps and develop the right messaging for new audiences. Create a new persona and distinct positioning so you can launch messages that cut through and motivate this new set of customers. Most times your brand personality will stay the same, but you may tailor your tone to this new customer segment.

Your top competitors shift. When you see that your ideal customers start considering different competitors, it's time to refresh your messaging. The messages you use to stand out from a new set of competitors will likely be different from your existing messaging. Also, when your current competitors introduce attractive new benefits and features, you'll want to make sure your value propositions still make your product shine.

You launch major product changes. As your product transforms through new feature releases, acquisitions, or partnerships, you may be able to promise even better benefits. When you introduce game-changing new product capabilities, your old messaging may undersell your product's value. Your persona and positioning may shift, and you may even need to adjust your brand personality to reflect these changes. In these cases, you'll develop value propositions and proof points that introduce exciting new reasons to choose your product.

Now that you understand how and when to update your 3 Ps, you'll want to embrace several helpful mindsets as you move through the messaging development process.

EMBRACE THESE MESSAGING MINDSETS

You probably have questions going into this process, especially as a leader of an early stage startup where your resources are lean, time is tight, and growth goals are ambitious.

"I have to move quickly. Do we really need to do all the steps in this book?"

"I don't have a marketing team yet. Can I actually accomplish this work?"

"Our product is changing so quickly. What if our messaging becomes outdated again?"

If any of these questions are going through your head, I have good news for you: This book gives you an efficient process to develop high-performing product messaging, even with a lean (or no) marketing team. This is a process you'll go through over and over again, so invest in learning it early to guide more effective business decisions through the many stages of your startup's growth.

When you embrace several key mindsets, you'll be able to move more quickly and make more effective decisions. You'll likely speed through some of the steps in this book but feel like other parts are a stretch. These three mindsets will help you navigate hang-ups and get the most out of the process.

Create value for customers. The success of messaging and marketing is rooted in creating value for your ideal customers. Make your persona (which you'll develop over the next two chapters) the filter for all your messaging decisions. This book gives you the tools to develop the empathy and the messages that connect with the people who need your product. When you know how your ideal customer thinks, you can explain your product in a way that builds trust and validates your claims. For every message you create, ask yourself, "Will this motivate my persona? Is this information useful and appealing to them?" If not, scrap it and develop messaging that resonates instead.

Embrace the iterative process. Learn and get comfortable with the messaging development process so you can iterate as your market evolves. The steps you take to understand your ideal customers' needs and your competitive advantage are foundational to your marketing strategy. Don't think of messaging development as a "one-and-done" process. Instead, embrace it as an iterative process you'll repeat as your product's value and differentiators shift. Be ready to make tweaks anytime something significant changes in your market and you need to rethink your messaging.

Have a bias toward action. Don't get stuck in any step of this process. Take the best information you have and be hypothesis-driven to avoid stalling out at any point. You won't truly know what messages drive customer action until you test them. You'll learn more from getting feedback on your new messaging in real-world scenarios than researching and refining it week after week on a screen. That also creates less pressure on your team to make the messaging "perfect." Launch and see actual user behavior to inform your decisions. The toolkit found in this book helps you update your content and marketing touchpoints, knowing you'll refine over time.

Defining your 3 Ps is an iterative process, so plan to launch, learn, and refine. You'll make the most progress if you put your ideal customer's needs at the center of all decisions. To help you do that, let's dive into the first P: creating your ICP and personas.

STANDOUT STRATEGIES:

‣ Define your 3 Ps—persona, positioning, and personality—to gain the insights you need to develop effective product messaging.

‣ Recognize when you'll need to update product messaging as your ideal customer, product, and market evolve.

‣ Embrace several important mindsets to make the messaging development process run more smoothly. Put your ideal customer at the center of decisions, iterate as needed, and have a bias towards action.

CHAPTER 2

DECIDE WHO YOU ARE TALKING TO

Sophia, the founder of a security software platform that detects risks for e-commerce companies, asked me to review her startup's website. The website was freshly redesigned, and it was beautiful: full of inspiring graphics, modern fonts, logos from top VC investors, and detailed descriptions of their product features. From their homepage, I was also able to download a report that validated the merits of their product's approach to monitoring security threats.

But there was a clear messaging gap. The website talked about what "we" do and shared information about the company, its product, and its features. It was a product brochure that made their functionality the focus of the content rather than putting their ideal customer at the center of the story. As I read through the website, it was not clear what types of companies would be a good fit for their product or what outcomes their customers achieved with the product. There were no customer success stories to validate that their product was effective. While the downloadable report had lots of facts about the product's new technology, it didn't answer the customer's main questions: *"Who is this product for? What could it do for me?"*

"Your website needs to talk directly to your ideal user, showing that you understand their challenges and what they want to accomplish," I told Sophia. "It needs to emphasize that you have a solution that delivers the results their business needs. It's also important to explain why your product is better than any of the other solutions they could choose to address their company's security issues. Right now, your website only talks about your product and your company. It's not talking to anyone specifically, and it's not helping your ideal customer make a decision."

For startups, the first step of the product messaging process is to decide exactly who you are speaking to. If you sell to businesses, what types of companies are your best-fit customers? Within those companies, who is your ideal customer? What is their decision-making process? To define this, you'll create an ideal customer profile (ICP) to describe the business you sell to. Then you'll define the exact person you're talking to in your messaging and capture their needs, desires, and motivations in a persona. If you sell a product directly to consumers, you'll skip creating an ICP and move straight to creating your persona.

Your persona becomes the filter for all your messaging choices. It captures what a customer values as they consider a solution like yours. Once you know these insights, your team can shift from "we" messaging (telling the story of your product and company) to "you" messaging (speaking directly to your ideal customer about how your product can help them). This is the type of messaging that motivates your ideal customer to learn about, buy, and use your product. It explains what your product enables them to accomplish in their life or business.

One of the biggest mistakes startup leaders make is using the same messaging to try to appeal to multiple types of customers, who each have different needs and motivations. When you create messaging for a generic group, you rarely address an individual's specific struggles and desires. Instead, you need to decide exactly who you're talking to, create messaging that empathizes with that person's needs, and promise to deliver the results they want most.

In B2B (business-to-business) startups, when you use the same messaging to talk to everyone involved in the buying decision at your ICP company, your messaging will also fall flat. You need to understand each person's role and vantage point so you can address their specific needs and thought processes. Messaging that you develop for a persona will focus on exactly what that person cares about, and this will build trust and desire. Your ideal customers will quickly see that you understand their unique needs, and you will help them decide that your product is their best choice.

If your startup is B2C (business-to-consumer), you can now move straight into creating a persona of the ideal person who will buy and use your product. Head to chapter 3 to get started. For B2B companies, it's time to create your ICP and then identify the key people involved in the buying process for your product (your "buying committee"). Then you'll create a persona for each of those individuals, starting with your "primary buyer." That will enable you to craft customized messages for each persona.

CREATE YOUR IDEAL CUSTOMER PROFILE

It's time to describe the type of company that needs a solution like yours. What are the specific characteristics of companies with challenges that your product solves well? What type of company benefits most from your product? What happens within these companies that leads them to need a solution like yours? You'll capture this in an ideal customer profile (you can use the template at the end of this chapter).

Capture these characteristics in your ICP:

✦ **Firmographics:** factors including industry, size, revenue, number of employees, and business model

✦ **Technographics:** factors including current technology stack, budget, tech mindset, and team structure

✦ **Pains:** the painful challenges and/or unrealized opportunities that the company faces

✦ **Gains:** the desirable results or outcomes that the company needs once it overcomes the pains

✦ **Shifts:** the changes or events that make the company open to finding a solution to the pains

As a B2B startup, you likely have a sales team that frequently talks to your ideal customers. It's critical that you partner with sales team members to develop your ICP and personas. They will have invaluable insights to help you determine which companies are the best fit for your product. Plus they have direct access to the exact people they sell your product to within those companies. Working with your sales team also allows you to create a shared understanding across marketing and sales, which will lead to more coordinated messaging and content efforts. Work together to fast-track the creation of these profiles.

With clarity on your ICP, you'll then identify the people on the buying committee who will decide whether to buy and use your product. People on your buying committee often include:

+ **Primary buyer:** the main person who leads the process to evaluate and get buy-in for your product

+ **Decision maker:** the person who makes the final decision about whether to buy your product

+ **Influencers:** people who help establish the use cases, evaluate options, and inform the buying decision

+ **User:** the end user of the product after purchase

Once you identify these key players, first create a persona of the primary buyer. This is the central person you need to understand and motivate right away with your messaging and content. Then, for the other people who play an influential role in the buying process but have different pains, gains, and shifts, you'll create additional personas. Then you'll craft a customized messaging framework for each persona.

As I worked through this process with Sophia, it was clear that she knew her ICP well. Her inspiration for starting the company came from leading engineering teams at two different mid-sized e-commerce companies that had struggled to find the right security solution for their sites. She had first-hand experience with the security risks that these companies faced and the pressures the teams felt. She also knew how to develop the exact product they needed to solve these pain points.

Once Sophia developed her ICP summary, it was time to define the company's buying committee. While the ICP is a synopsis of the company's issues, messaging needs to motivate the specific people who evaluate, buy, and use the product. So the founder's next step was to define exactly who her team would talk to through their messaging. Her list included:

- ✦ **Primary buyer:** an engineering director, who is tasked with managing the e-commerce site's security

- ✦ **Decision maker:** the CEO, who is accountable for revenue for the company

- ✦ **Influencers:** the heads of product and customer success, who manage the site's shopping experience

- ✦ **User:** an engineer on the engineering director's team who would use the software every day

The primary buyer at their ICP was an engineering leader who felt pulled in many directions. Monitoring site security was urgent, but it wasn't the type of work that the company's engineers wanted to do. They'd rather be making more exciting customer-facing updates to their sites. Time spent monitoring threats and dealing with security breaches felt like a distraction and nuisance. The teams also felt vulnerable because they often lacked the specialized expertise needed to monitor security risks. They feared that they'd miss a threat or struggle to fix a security incident if it occurred. That would be bad for the business and their jobs.

The ICP leadership team's two biggest concerns were downtime and customer data breaches. Security incidents could obliterate trust with customers, tank revenue, and cause major disruptions to fulfillment. What type of solution did these companies want most? They needed a highly reliable, easy-to-manage security platform. The software needed to proactively detect security threats to their shopping site and quickly identify the root cause of issues when they happened. The solution also needed to be affordable and easy for the ICP's lean engineering teams to implement.

With this information, Sophia was ready to move into creating a persona for her primary buyer. She knew that the engineering director was the most important person to start with. The director researched security solutions and steered the process to decide which one to select for their company. You'll find all the steps to create your own persona in chapter 3.

STANDOUT STRATEGIES:

‣ Decide exactly who you're talking to in your marketing collateral and sales pitch as a starting point for defining effective messaging.

‣ Rely on your persona as a filter for all messaging decisions. Every message needs to speak to and resonate with one specific person, not a generic group.

‣ Create an ICP (if you're a B2B startup), which describes the company that is your ideal customer. Then determine who's on the buying committee, including the "primary buyer," who will be the subject of your first persona.

IDEAL CUSTOMER PROFILE (ICP) TEMPLATE

FIRMOGRAPHICS

Describe the characteristics of the ideal company that will buy and use your product.

- ✦ Industry, size:
- ✦ Geography, locations:
- ✦ Number of employees, company structure:
- ✦ Revenue, business model:

TECHNOGRAPHICS

Describe the technology setup and prerequisites that your ideal company needs.

- ✦ Tech stack, systems, budget:
- ✦ Team members:
- ✦ Mindsets:

PAINS

Describe the challenges this company experiences that your product can solve. List in order of frustration and importance to solve.

- ✦ 1
- ✦ 2
- ✦ 3

GAINS

Describe the results this company desires once it overcomes these pains. List in order of impact and importance to achieve.

- ✦ 1
- ✦ 2
- ✦ 3

SHIFTS

Describe the changes or events that make this company's team realize they have a problem and need a solution.

- ✦ 1
- ✦ 2
- ✦ 3

CHAPTER 3

CAPTURE YOUR PERSONA

Now that you know exactly who you need to talk to in your messaging, it's time to create a persona. Personas summarize what your ideal customer values, the challenges they face, and the results they desire. They also detail what's holding your ideal customers back from addressing their pain points, and what will motivate them to move forward and choose a solution.

Personas are a shortcut to building empathy. They capture the insights you need to create messaging that speaks to your ideal customers about what matters to them. Base your persona on an actual person who's had an outstanding experience with your product and achieved great results. Picture the circumstances that led them to your product: their lifestyle, work situation, unmet needs, and aspirations. To develop your persona, capture what they say, think, feel, and do about the problems your product solved for them. When you create your messaging, you'll write as if you're talking or communicating directly with this person.

Less-useful personas capture demographics (a person's external and statistical characteristics) and psychographics (a person's general mindsets and worldviews). These factors may help you identify and target a group of similar people through your marketing and sales efforts. But they don't tell you much at all about how a specific person discovers, evaluates, and selects products like yours. A useful persona for messaging captures someone's specific use cases, including their needs and desires related to the pain points your product solves.

To build an effective messaging persona, you'll need to describe these five factors about your ideal customer:

✦ **Pains:** the painful challenges or unrealized opportunities that your persona faces

✦ **Gains:** the desirable results or outcomes that your persona seeks, leading to a transformation

✦ **Shift:** the changes or events that create a need for your persona to address the pains

✦ **Blockers:** the concerns, hang-ups, and objections your persona has about choosing a solution

✦ **Motivators:** the enticing benefits, proof points, and influencers that drive your persona to take action

A persona helps you understand the transformation journey that your product and marketing create for your ideal customer. In a persona, you'll capture your ideal customer's starting point (pains) and desired endpoint (gains). You'll describe the event or change that makes your persona realize they have a pain that needs a solution (shift). Even then, objections inevitably hold your ideal customer back from choosing a solution (blockers), while certain information and influencers encourage your persona to move forward (motivators). Your next step is to create a persona that captures these five essential factors, and you'll find a template at the end of the chapter. Let's dive in.

EMPATHIZE WITH THEIR PAINS

To relate to your ideal customer through your messaging, you'll need to understand their most urgent and powerful pain points and their unrealized desires. In your messaging, you'll present your product as a bridge leading out of their pain and into the gain.

Powerful messaging addresses the functional tasks that your ideal customer needs a product to accomplish. Importantly, it also speaks to the emotional and social challenges that your persona wants to overcome. Your ideal customer's pains fall into three categories:

✦ **Functional:** jobs to be done and tasks your persona wants to accomplish

✦ **Emotional:** feelings and internal thoughts your persona wants to overcome

✦ **Social:** relationships and external perceptions your persona wants to improve

In your persona template, list the pain points that your ideal customer faces. Capture the most important tasks they need to accomplish under "functional" pains. Then consider how your persona feels in their current state, and list their "emotional" pains too. Do they feel helpless, frustrated, confused, overwhelmed, angry, tense, concerned, fearful, or something else? For "social" pains, identify what's strained in their relationships and how they want to be perceived by others in more positive ways, too. Many times, someone's biggest underlying motivation to solve a problem is not just to get jobs done. It's to eliminate negative feelings and external friction that are holding them back.

Sophia, the e-commerce security platform's founder, first created the persona of her primary buyer, the engineering director responsible for their company's website security. This director struggled with catching security threats before they impacted sales and the customer shopping experience. The engineering director also knew that their team dreaded monitoring and fixing security issues, so the lack of a user-friendly solution impacted employee engagement and retention. Sophia captured the director's pains in a persona:

PAINS: ENGINEERING DIRECTOR

+ **Functional:** difficult to identify and catch security vulnerabilities, lack of expertise on their lean team, risk of site downtime and significant lost sales, potential harm to customers if a security breach occurs

+ **Emotional:** worried about the effectiveness of their current approach, anxious about asking their team to monitor security rather than build features, fearful of consequences if a security breach occurs

+ **Social:** reputation risk if a security breach occurs, pressure from the C-suite to get site security under control, risk of losing team members who don't enjoy security monitoring work

Once you've identified your persona's pain points, you can determine which challenges matter most to them by creating a *pain point graph*. The horizontal axis represents your persona's level of frustration or the intensity of their pain. The vertical axis represents the potential impact or the importance of resolving that pain. When you plot each of your persona's functional, emotional, and social pains on this graph, you'll see how they compare. The highest priority pain points will be in the upper right of the graph. These are the pain points you'll want to include in your messaging because your customer needs to solve them above all else. This messaging is also more likely to catch the customer's attention.

PAIN POINT GRAPH: ENGINEERING DIRECTOR

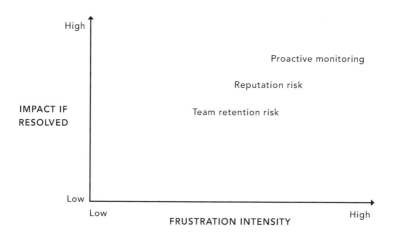

Sophia confirmed that having a reliable platform that proactively detected security risks was her buyer's top functional need. She also realized that solving the engineering director's most intense social pains would have a high impact. These included (1) reputation risk if a security breach occurred and (2) retention risk of losing team members if they had to continue to perform security monitoring work. To show that her platform could resolve these issues, Sophia needed to understand what her persona wanted to experience if they could eliminate these pains. This is what she captured in the "gains" section of her persona, which is your next step, too.

DISCOVER THEIR DESIRED GAINS

Once you understand your persona's pains, it's time to map out their desired gains. What are the outcomes your persona wants to experience once they overcome their top challenges? In your list of gains, don't stop until you understand the ultimate reason that your persona wants to resolve their pains. Keep asking *"Why does that matter to them?"* This will help you understand the end outcome you need to promise in your messaging to speak to your persona's goals on a functional, emotional, and social level.

To uncover the reason a gain matters to your ideal customer, you can ask:

+ What is the ultimate outcome or change my persona wants to achieve?

+ What is the most significant reason the outcome matters to my persona?

+ Why is this improvement or transformation important to my persona?

Many times, the gain someone wants most will improve their life in one of these four categories: health, wealth, self, or relationships. Functional benefits have emotional value. Identify the positive emotions your persona will experience as your solution delivers results. They may feel joyful, relieved, respected, empowered, skilled, confident, attractive, or in control. Effective messaging helps your persona envision a life where the positive outcomes are achievable and rewarding. Capture insights about your persona's gains so you can craft meaningful messages that speak to their desired future.

Looking back at her persona's pain points, Sophia saw a clear list of "jobs to be done" that an engineering director needed from software that protected their site's security. Sophia also realized that the engineering director wanted to have a thriving career and to be known as a capable engineering leader who could retain a highly engaged team. The director's current method for monitoring security threats put these goals in jeopardy. Why did this matter? Poor job performance could impact their career trajectory (wealth), company earnings (wealth), personal sense of well-being and growth (self), and team happiness (relationships). Sophia included these desired gains in the persona template:

GAINS: ENGINEERING DIRECTOR

✦ **Functional:** a solution that can catch vulnerabilities before there's a security breach, rapidly alert the team when breaches occur, identify the root cause of breaches so the team can address them quickly

✦ **Emotional:** comfort that the site has best-in-class monitoring, confidence that they'll detect and address any breach quickly, relief that the team has security under control, excitement to free up their team's time

✦ **Social:** team is known and respected for maintaining a safe and reliable site, manager is seen as a valuable and effective company leader, team is highly engaged and focused on work to increase sales

Sophia realized that the engineering director wanted control over data security without their team needing to be hands-on or bogged down in the day-to-day details. The engineering leader put company outcomes first, knowing a data breach was detrimental to customers, company revenue, and their career. The director also wanted to empower their team to do more interesting work that increased happiness and retention. Plus the director cared about their career advancement and could not let any security issues slip through. These nuances became important inputs for the startup's messaging.

RECOGNIZE THE SHIFTS THEY EXPERIENCE

How does someone go from not needing your product one day to being actively interested the next? This happens when your persona experiences a "shift," the inciting incident in their journey from pain to gain. The shift is the set of events or changes that happen in your ideal customer's personal or professional life that makes them realize "*I have a problem.*" The shift may be gradual, or it may be an event that creates an immediate need to fix the pain point. Even if your persona has ignored a latent pain for a while, the shift will create urgency and spur them to action.

Understanding the shifts your persona encounters will reveal what's happening in their life or business at the time they need your product. Your messaging will be timelier and more relevant if it speaks to what your persona is experiencing once your product catches their attention. The shift will also shed light on your persona's mindset and level of urgency to solve the pain. You'll understand what's creating pressure for them to act and what other stakeholders are involved, too.

When Sophia dug into her persona's shift, she realized that the e-commerce engineering director often managed with a suboptimal security solution until external pressure caused them to change. The director usually had a non-expert team member monitoring their site for security risks, relying on the basic security controls their site's platform offered or a system they built in-house. This was a ticking time bomb.

What made the engineering director suddenly open to considering a stronger solution? For most leaders in this position, one of two events caused the shift:

1. Their e-commerce site experienced a security breach that significantly impacted the business, costing revenue, customers, and time. The CEO sent a clear "never again" message to the engineering director, and they immediately began evaluating solutions.

2. The CEO proactively asked the engineering director to find a better security solution, either because they'd experienced a damaging security breach at a previous company or because of a mandate from the company's board of directors. In this case, the engineering director might feel like the stakes were high, but they hadn't yet been burned by a breach.

To identify your persona's shifts, ask these questions:

✦ What signs make your persona realize they have a problem to solve?

✦ When does this shift usually occur? What events precede this shift? What happens next?

✦ What does your persona experience and feel when this shift occurs?

✦ How urgent is solving the problem once the shift happens?

The shift makes your persona more open to hearing about a solution like yours. It also creates pressure and tension, so it's helpful to know what's happening in the background as they research, evaluate, and select a solution. Get specific about the shift so that your messaging can speak to exactly what's going on in that person's life or business. And no matter how pressing it is for your persona to find a solution, there will still be obstacles to taking action. That's what you'll capture in the "blockers" section of your persona template.

IDENTIFY THEIR BLOCKERS

Even when someone knows they need to solve a problem, they may feel reluctant to find or choose a solution. You need to proactively address your persona's objections to help them take action. Blockers could be negative mindsets, lack of trust in the results, financial limitations, time constraints, or social pressure, among other things. What stops your persona from considering a solution in the first place? Once they start evaluating solutions and your product is on their list, what are their main objections to buying *your* product? Summarize these insights in the "blockers" section of your persona template.

The e-commerce engineering director faces a range of blockers, even after the shift occurs. These include:

+ It's time-consuming and distracting to research and evaluate solutions.

+ They often don't feel confident about how to select the right platform.

+ There's a risk in relying on external software, so they consider building a solution in-house.

+ They need buy-in from multiple people before they can purchase a solution (see the "buying committee" in chapter 2).

Sophia learned several important things from these insights. First, the engineering director didn't know how to effectively evaluate the security platform options on the market. The director was worried about "reputation risk" and the impact on the business if they selected the wrong platform. The stakes were high. Sophia needed to help the director understand how to evaluate platforms, show that her startup's product was their best choice, and help them convince the buying committee, too. Sophia captured what would help move the director past their blockers in the final part of the persona: "motivators."

UNDERSTAND THEIR MOTIVATORS

What will your ideal customer need to see, hear, or experience to believe your product is the best solution for them? How can you prove your product's ability to deliver the desired gains? In the "motivators" section of your persona template, note the types of information and the people that your ideal customer trusts to help them make a decision. These could include customer success stories, data, endorsements, or even demos that let them experience the product. You'll learn all about effective proof points in chapter 9.

With her persona's blockers in mind, Sophia realized that testimonials from other engineering leaders at similar companies would help. The startup needed to showcase the security platform's positive impact on businesses that were similar to the engineering director's company. Plus, Sophia needed to educate engineering directors on what to look for in an effective security software platform, then show how their product delivered on these dimensions. Data about uptime, threats avoided, and speed to resolve security breaches would give the engineering manager comfort that the product could accomplish their goals.

With her ICP and persona completed, Sophia had a clear idea of what she needed to communicate to her ideal customers. When you know the five factors of your persona, you understand what your ideal customer values and the results they want most. You can create messaging that speaks directly to their mindsets and motivations, helping them feel confident that they'll achieve their goals.

Once you've completed your persona, you're ready to move to the next step of developing effective messaging: understanding what differentiates your product from the competition.

STANDOUT STRATEGIES:

‣ Describe your persona's pains and desired gains, including functional (jobs to be done), emotional (feelings), and social (relationships and perceptions).

‣ Understand the shifts that your persona experiences, making them aware of their pain points and open to finding a solution to their problem.

‣ Anticipate your persona's biggest blockers and objections to choosing a solution like yours, then determine what motivators help overcome these concerns.

PERSONA TEMPLATE

DEMOGRAPHICS (OPTIONAL)

Describe the profile characteristics of your ideal customer.

- ✦ Age, gender:
- ✦ Location:
- ✦ Education, career path:
- ✦ Lifestyle:

ROLE (ADD TO B2B PERSONAS)

Describe the professional characteristics of your ideal customer.

- ✦ Job title, success metrics:
- ✦ Who they report to (manager), who reports to them (direct reports):
- ✦ Career aspirations:
- ✦ Role challenges:

PAINS

Describe the challenges your ideal customer experiences that your product can solve. List in order of importance.

- ✦ Functional (jobs to be done and tasks to accomplish):
- ✦ Emotional (feelings and internal thoughts):
- ✦ Social (relationships and external perceptions):

GAINS

Describe the results your ideal customer desires once they overcome these pains. List in order of importance.

- ✦ Functional (jobs to be done and tasks to accomplish):
- ✦ Emotional (feelings and internal thoughts):
- ✦ Social (relationships and external perceptions):

SHIFTS

Describe the changes or events that make your ideal customer realize they have a problem and need a solution.

- ✦ 1
- ✦ 2
- ✦ 3

BLOCKERS

Describe the objections that prevent your ideal customer from taking action to solve their pains.

- 1
- 2
- 3

MOTIVATORS

Describe the proof points that motivate your ideal customers to move forward and select a solution.

- 1
- 2
- 3

CHANNELS

Describe where you can find, reach, and connect with your ideal customers.

- Influencers, trusted sources:
- Publications, blogs, social media:
- Associations, communities:
- Events:
- Online channels:

CHAPTER 4

UNDERSTAND THE COMPETITION

Your persona is your go-to guide for what your ideal customer values. That means you now have the keys to explain your product in terms that resonate with your ideal customer's needs. But what makes your product *more* valuable and attractive than the other solutions your ideal customer could choose?

The next step toward powerful product messaging is to identify your product's most appealing and distinctive differentiators. Once you know what makes your product stand out, you'll create product positioning that summarizes how your product is different and better than any other solution. Your positioning defines your unique competitive advantage and succinctly shares why your ideal customer should choose your product over others.

As a first step, you'll create a *competitive map* that compares your product to competing solutions. You'll identify your top competitors and then determine why your persona is attracted to each solution. You'll also pinpoint why the results your product delivers, and the user experience it offers, are better for your ideal customer than the alternatives. Those insights will ensure your messaging reflects your competitive edge. Let's dive in.

IDENTIFY YOUR COMPETITOR SHORTLIST

Now that you know your persona, you can identify what products and solutions your ideal customer considers to solve their challenges. These may be well-established companies, other startups, or point solutions that your persona pieces together. Sometimes your competitors will surprise you; they're not always the obvious other products in your market. Think beyond direct competitors and consider the range of ways your persona may address their challenges. Your persona may choose to build a solution in-house, manage a process manually with a spreadsheet, or do the work with pen and paper. Strong messaging ensures your product stands out above any of the other options that your persona seriously considers.

"We've realized that if we don't close a sale, we're usually not losing customers to our direct 'tech platform' competitors," Lucas, the CEO and cofounder of a startup recruiting platform, told me. "Today, all of our messaging talks about why we're better than the other well-known recruiting platforms in our space. That means we're missing messages that show how our product is better than the services our ideal customers choose most often." It was clear that Lucas needed to figure out how to define and understand his product's competitive landscape.

Lucas's startup offered a platform for companies to find and contract with freelance recruiters who specialize in hiring for specific types of roles. The startup's ICP was a growth-stage company that needed to hire at least 20 new employees within a year and wanted to work with specialized recruiters. But these companies did not have the time or budget to hire a team of recruiting specialists. Through the recruiting startup's platform, companies could quickly start working with the exact recruiters they needed without needing to scale their own team in-house.

The startup's "primary buyer" persona, a head of recruiting who managed hiring across all functions at the ICP company, usually defaulted to building their own recruiting team. But their in-house team often consisted of generalist recruiters, who could not close candidates in each function as effectively as specialists. In other cases, the head of recruiting would hire a recruiting firm. But these agencies were often expensive, and it could feel overwhelming to hire and manage multiple specialized agencies.

Lucas also knew that two competing tech platforms offered access to specialized recruiters. But no other platform offered the breadth of recruiting specialists that Lucas's platform did. Most of the startup's messaging talked about why their platform was better than these other tech solutions. But Lucas knew the startup also needed to explain why their platform was more effective than hiring an agency or building an in-house team. That's where they were losing sales.

As a next step, Lucas created a competitive map. To create your competitive map, put together a shortlist of the top three to five alternative solutions that your ideal customer considers to solve their pains. These are the solutions that your persona will be comparing your product to as they read your website, enter a sales conversation, and decide which solution to choose. Leave out the products that your persona doesn't evaluate or use, even if they're considered the top products in your category.

Competitive alternatives may include:

✦ **Direct competitors:** products that solve similar problems in similar ways to your product

✦ **Indirect competitors:** products that solve similar problems in different ways than your product

✦ **Do-it-yourself (DIY):** solutions that solve similar problems and are built in-house or are manual

✦ **Do nothing:** the choice not to solve the problem right now

The freelance recruiting platform's shortlist included:

✦ **Direct competitors:** Two other platforms offered access to freelance, specialized recruiters. Each platform offered recruiters for a single function: one for sales teams, the other for hiring engineers.

✦ **Indirect competitors:** Recruiting firms were their most formidable indirect competitors. Some agencies recruited for a broad range of roles, while others focused on hiring talent for a narrow set of functions.

✦ **Do-it-yourself:** Their persona's most common alternative was to hire an in-house team to manage recruiting for roles across the company. They often hired generalists rather than specialists.

✦ **Do nothing:** This was not an option for their ICP, since these companies needed to hire at least 20 people per year. It was essential for their ICP to have recruiting support to meet their hiring goals.

Note that some of these competitors are products, and some are not. This is why I call competitive alternatives "solutions." It's a reminder that, sometimes, your most challenging competition is not another tech product, and this will significantly impact your messaging.

CREATE A COMPETITIVE MAP

Once you have a shortlist of competitors, you need to identify what makes each product or solution enticing to your ideal customer. Your competitive map captures the unique advantages of using each solution. Differentiators fall into two main buckets:

+ **Benefits:** the positive outcomes and results the solution delivers for customers

+ **Functionality:** how the solution works and the features that solve customers' challenges

When your product differentiates on *benefits*, it delivers more attractive results for customers than the competitive solutions do. Your product achieves better outcomes and may also address the root cause of the pain points in a more effective way. When you differentiate on *functionality*, you help customers achieve similar outcomes as competing products but with a better user experience.

To fill in your competitive map, first identify the benefits and functionality each solution on your list has in common. Then you'll summarize what sets each solution apart. Use the *competitive map* template at the end of this chapter.

Common characteristics. First, note the set of benefits and functionality that you *and* your competitors offer. For your ideal customer to consider a solution, what benefits does it need to offer? What features do your ideal customers expect each solution to include? These are your persona's table-stakes requirements for the top solutions they consider. Outline these in your *common characteristics* list.

Differentiated characteristics. Next, identify each solution's most compelling differentiators. Your goal is to understand what makes your ideal customer choose one solution vs. another. Why is each solution uniquely effective and desirable? What is each solution's X-factor that makes it a top choice for your persona? Since you already know what your persona values most, you'll be able to identify what attracts them to your competitors. In your competitive map, outline the *differentiated characteristics* of each solution, including yours.

Top differentiators. Now, look back at the unique characteristics you listed for each of your competitors. Summarize the top two to three differentiators that sway your persona towards choosing each option. Then, look at *your* product and list the two to three differentiators that help it win against the alternatives. These insights give you strong hints about how to favorably position your product, which we'll cover in chapter 6.

Differentiators heat map. You can turn this *top differentiators* list into a heat map that visually shows which solution is most appealing to your ideal customer. Look at the top differentiators list for your competitors and your product. Highlight the most attractive differentiators in green and the next most attractive set in yellow.

Look across the dashboard to see which solutions have the most green and yellow, and you'll see at a glance why your persona prefers one option over another. The green differentiators likely address your persona's most acute pains or desirable gains. A product with more green highlights stands out for its unique advantages.

How did the competitive map look when Lucas's startup captured how their primary buyer, the head of recruiting, regarded top alternatives? Here's the summary:

RECRUITING PLATFORM COMPETITIVE MAP

COMMON CHARACTERISTICS

✦ **Common benefits:** create a high-quality pipeline of candidates for open roles, increase close rates through recruiters' specialized expertise, make recruiting as effortless as possible for hiring managers

✦ **Common functionality:** enable sourcing of candidates, track applicants, manage communications with candidates, record interview notes, score candidates, create offers, analyze and report on pipeline

DIFFERENTIATED CHARACTERISTICS

✦ **Direct competitors:** platforms offering specialized, freelance recruiters

- The most recruiters in a specific function (one platform for sales, one platform for engineering)
- More integrations with recruiting sites, so perceived access to a higher volume of candidates

✦ **Indirect competitor:** hire a recruiting firm

- Fully managed experience from an agency that handles all aspects of recruiting
- Maintain flexibility without hiring full-time specialized recruiters

✦ **Do-it-yourself solution:** hire a team of recruiters in-house

- Not locked into contracts and easier to reallocate recruiters to new roles as hiring needs change
- Seamless communication between the in-house team and hiring managers to make decisions faster

✦ **Startup platform's differentiators**
- One-stop shop to find specialized recruiters for a range of functions
- Lower cost than recruiting firms, with the benefits and high close rates of specialized recruiters

This competitive map (paired with their persona) helped Lucas understand what made a head of recruiting choose one solution over the other. Ultimately, the recruiting leader's goal was to quickly hire high-quality candidates. But they also had to balance a limited budget, needed flexibility as hiring priorities changed, and desired specialized recruiters who closed candidates at a high rate. To stand out, Lucas's messaging needed to emphasize their platform's differentiators that delivered the right benefits and functionality.

After putting together your competitive map, you likely have strong insights about what makes your product the best possible choice for your ideal customers. That said, you probably still have some gaps in your persona template and your competitive map that research can help fill in. Now is the best time to clarify your understanding and develop these extra insights so that you can move into positioning with a clear point of view. Turn to the next chapter to learn about a range of easy-to-implement research techniques.

STANDOUT STRATEGIES:

▸ Identify a shortlist of solutions your persona will consider to solve their pain points. You'll identify what differentiates your product from these alternatives.

▸ Develop a competitive map that captures common and differentiated benefits and functionality that each solution offers.

▸ Summarize each solution's top differentiators that make it particularly attractive and appealing to your ideal customers. Clarify what makes your product stand out above the others.

COMPETITIVE MAP TEMPLATE

COMPETITOR LIST

List the competitive alternatives that your ideal customers use to solve their problems.

+ Direct competitors:
+ Indirect competitors:
+ DIY or manual solutions:

COMMON BENEFITS

What are the expected benefits that all these solutions deliver?

+ 1
+ 2
+ 3

COMMON FUNCTIONALITY

What are the expected features that all these solutions offer?

+ 1
+ 2
+ 3

DIFFERENTIATED CHARACTERISTICS

For your product and each of the competitors on your list, identify their differentiated (1) benefits and (2) functionality. What makes each solution stand out to your ideal customers? Why do they choose each product?

YOUR PRODUCT: ....

BENEFITS

What are the differentiated benefits that your product delivers?

+ 1
+ 2
+ 3

FUNCTIONALITY

What are the differentiated features that your product offers?

- 1
- 2
- 3

DIRECT COMPETITOR: _____

BENEFITS

What are the differentiated benefits that this solution delivers?

- 1
- 2
- 3

FUNCTIONALITY

What are the differentiated features that this solution offers?

- 1
- 2
- 3

INDIRECT COMPETITOR: _____

BENEFITS

What are the differentiated benefits that this solution delivers?

- 1
- 2
- 3

FUNCTIONALITY

What are the differentiated features that this solution offers?

- 1
- 2
- 3

CHAPTER 5

FILL IN GAPS
WITH RESEARCH

Doing rapid research will help you fill in any details you aren't sure about in your persona and competitive map. The best next step is to gather the missing insights and test your assumptions through customer and competitive research. Then you'll incorporate what you learn into a more polished version of your persona and competitive map. These will give you the insights you need to develop your positioning and personality in the next two chapters.

I worked with Caroline, the CEO and cofounder of an accounting software startup who knew her team had achieved product-market fit. But the startup's messaging was holding back its customer acquisition efforts. Their marketing collateral, including their website, email sequences, and even their onboarding guides, still reflected an early version of their product. Caroline's team had learned a lot about the small business owners who were the right fit for their product, but going through the persona-creation exercise sparked a lot of questions, too.

Caroline also felt unsure about her product's differentiators and wanted to determine whether their unique invoicing features gave their product an edge over competitors. So the team planned a couple of weeks of research to dig into these questions. They conducted customer interviews, gathered sales team insights, and employed a variety of other research methods, which you'll learn about next.

CONDUCT CUSTOMER INTERVIEWS

There's no substitute for talking directly to a set of your ideal customers to refine your persona and understanding of your top competitors. Plan to speak to a set of power users, less active users, and prospective customers who fit your ideal profile. Conducting customer interviews will allow you to notice patterns, synthesize themes, and choose one individual as the basis for your persona. Usually, you'll start to see consistent insights emerge after five interviews; conducting ten interviews often gives you a solid picture of your persona's mindsets.

   Who you interview depends on how clear you are about who your ideal customer is.

✦ **If you're still trying to figure out who your best-fit customer is:** Talk to a range of people in different customer segments to understand their unique needs and buying behavior. Decide which segment reflects your ideal customers, then do a second round of research with these individuals so you can develop a full persona for this segment.

✦ **If you know who your best-fit customer is but don't fully understand their needs:** Conduct a larger number of interviews and start by asking open-ended questions about each person's needs, desires, blockers, and motivators. Synthesize what you discover. You may want to do a second round of research to refine your insights.

✦ **If you know your best-fit customer very well:** It's still helpful to talk to customers and test your assumptions before you finalize your persona and competitive map. Ask for specific feedback on the information you've already captured in your drafts and refine them based on what you learn.

Caroline's startup fell into the second bucket: The team knew who their best-fit customer was but didn't have clarity on all of their persona's factors. Because of this, she and the team decided to do two rounds of customer interviews. In the first round, they talked to ten small business owners who were likely their best-fit customers. These included a mix of current satisfied customers, prospects who hadn't yet subscribed, and people who'd never heard of their product before.

The team developed an interview guide to help them understand more about each entrepreneur's challenges in their businesses and current approach to accounting. The research helped them identify the top solutions these entrepreneurs considered and used, including other leading accounting software apps and their own DIY accounting approaches.

Caroline's team confirmed that invoicing was a large pain point for these small business owners. Creating invoices, sending them on time with all the right details, and following up for payment were time-consuming tasks and directly impacted revenue. After one round of research, the team set up interviews with an additional five people to explore some of their new insights and messaging ideas. Questions in the second round were more specific as the team aimed to solidify changes to their persona and competitive map.

Once you've identified the people you need to talk to, create a question guide for the customer interviews. Ask open-ended questions, including follow-up questions to get deeper insights into why someone answers a certain way. Be open to surprises, and plan to incorporate discoveries into your persona and competitive map. Here are the types of questions you can ask your ideal customers to fill in the details you need. In the places noted [need], fill in a description of the pain points or opportunity that your product addresses. Caroline's team replaced [need] with "accounting."

CUSTOMER INTERVIEW QUESTIONS

✦ How do you approach and think about [need] today?
  · What tasks do you need to complete?
  · How does your current process make you feel?
  · How does your current process impact your life and relationships?

✦ What are your challenges with [need] today?

✦ What are your goals or desired outcomes related to [need] today?

✦ What solutions do you use to address [need] today?
  · What's appealing about these solutions? What works well?
  · What's missing or not ideal about these solutions?

✦ What made you realize you need a solution for [need]?
  · What changed in your life, job, or business?
  · What challenges became too important to ignore? Why?

✦ How do you find out about and research solutions for [need]?

+ What criteria do you use to select a solution for [need]?
  · What results matter most to you?
  · What functionality or aspects of the solution matter most to you?

+ If you could wave a magic wand, what would your ideal solution to [need] help you achieve?
  · What tasks would you accomplish?
  · How would it make you feel?
  · How would it improve your relationships?
  · How would it improve how you're perceived?
  · What would be better about current solutions?

These questions help you see what drives your ideal customers' decisions about what solution is best for them. Another perspective you need to incorporate into your research is insights from the sales team, which you can gather in parallel to your customer interviews.

GATHER SALES TEAM INSIGHTS

In B2B companies, your sales team holds a treasure trove of insights that you can use in the messaging development process. Sales talks to your ideal customers every day and rapidly tests what messages drive action. If you have a sales team, make them your partners from the very beginning in developing your personas and competitive map.

Capture their perspective on what creates urgency for your ideal customers to find a solution. Learn why your ideal buyers choose your product over the alternatives (and vice versa). Work with sales to create the shortlist of direct and indirect competitors to include on your competitive map. Then fill in the details together. Start by asking your sales team open-ended questions to get their candid insights on your customers and market.

SALES TEAM INTERVIEW QUESTIONS

✦ ICP and Persona Insights
  • What companies have a strong need for our solution? List ICP characteristics.
  • Who is on the buying committee at these companies? List the primary buyer, decision maker, influencers, and users.
  • Now let's focus on the primary buyer.
  • What are their top pain points today (functional, emotional, social)?
  • What are the most important gains they seek (functional, emotional, social)?
  • What are their biggest unmet needs today? Where do other solutions fall short?
  • What is the shift that makes them open to finding a solution like ours?
  • How do they learn about and evaluate potential solutions?
  • What are their main blockers to moving forward with a solution?
  • What are the main motivators that help them select a solution?
  • What creates urgency for them to make a decision?
  • What makes them most interested in our product?

✦ Competitive Insights
  • What alternative solutions does our persona consider?
  • Why do they choose each of these solutions? What makes each solution attractive?

- What are our persona's challenges or unmet needs when they use the other solutions?
- What are their main questions about our product and other solutions?
- What are the most attractive benefits that our product offers?
- How is our product different and better than each alternative solution?
- Where does the budget come from for this type of solution?
- What do they think is a reasonable amount to spend on a solution?

With these insights, you'll have a complete picture of who your persona is and how they perceive your product versus competitors. You can also layer on other lightweight research methods to collect more details from different perspectives.

TAP OTHER RESEARCH METHODS

While customer and sales team interviews create a strong baseline, there are many other sources of information you can tap, too. Consider these research options and then choose the ones that are most feasible and relevant for your startup.

Customer support listening. Customer support teams and account managers are also very close to your ideal customer. They can help you understand what your users like most about your product and the results they're most excited to achieve. They can also fill you in on customers' frustrations, including what things confuse them about your product and what drives support calls. These team members' knowledge of what delights your active customers can also give you hints about your top differentiators.

Social listening. How customers talk about your product and brand on social media will give you insight into what they care about. First, mine comments on your own social media accounts to see what people are talking about: their challenges, desires, and perceptions of your product and other solutions. Then read through comments on your competitors' accounts and in communities where your ideal customers meet. See what pain points or frustrations people highlight, what solutions they're using, and what's working (or not). Note what gets rave reviews and what your ideal customers love most about your product and other solutions. Also, note where your product and the alternatives are letting down your ideal customers.

Customer data. Tap any sources of customer data you have for additional insights. Look through past survey responses that reveal how your ideal customer thinks. Revisit the results of net promoter score (NPS) surveys and other feedback that users submit through your app. Look at customer product usage data. Consider which features are used and talked about most often and which ones are underutilized. What do customers say they like most about your product? What do you wish more users knew about to increase their satisfaction with the product?

Competitive research. There's a lot you can learn from visiting your competitors' websites, consuming their content, and noticing their key messages. You can infer their ideal customer, the benefits and features they emphasize, and the way they build credibility. Check out their recent press coverage, feature launches, and their support content to understand what these companies do to create value for their customers. You'll also clarify how your product is different from theirs.

Keyword research. Once your ideal customer has a problem to solve, they often turn to search engines to research their symptoms, challenges, and possible solutions. There are many online tools that can help you identify highly-searched keywords and what sites rank in these searches. You'll learn what specific phrases people use in their searches too. When you see what terms drive high search volume, and what content ranks, you'll get a good sense of what your ideal customers learn in their research.

Survey. A survey will help you gather input from a large number of your ideal customers in a short period. You can ask participants to rank or share information on their needs, desires, shifts, motivators, and solutions they consider. You can also ask about what benefits and features they value most from a product like yours. Note that it's often easier to run a survey for a consumer product than for a B2B product, because it's harder to reach enough of a specific persona within your ICP.

After considering these tactics, Caroline dove into competitive research, reading through all the content she could find on competitors' accounting software sites to see what they highlighted as their differentiators. The team also launched a survey to get more input on what their persona needed in an accounting solution, how they evaluated products, and how they perceived each top competitor. Caroline became even more confident that their product's "magical" invoicing experience addressed a top customer pain point and set their startup apart from other products. Taking the time to collect these extra insights gave the team momentum and clarity as they moved into the positioning process (up ahead in chapter 6).

You can answer so many questions through these research methods, including:

✦ Unmet needs
- What are your ideal customers searching for to solve their problems?
- What pain points do they struggle to solve?
- What's disappointing about the current solutions they consider?
- What are the key challenges new users mention? What about ongoing active users?

✦ Value
- What are the main results or outcomes your ideal customer is looking for?
- What are their functional, emotional, and social pains and desired gains?
- What delights people about your product? What about competitors' products?

✦ Differentiation
- How do customers describe your product? What's appealing (or not)?
- What do customers think is different and better about your product?
- How do customers describe your competitors' brands and products? What's appealing (or not)?
- What do customers think is different and better about your competitors' products?
- Why does your ideal customer choose one solution over the others?

After completing your research, you can confidently update your persona and competitive map with new insights. At this point, you have the inputs you need to craft strong positioning that ensures your product stands out to your ideal customers. Turn to chapter 6 to find out how to define a favorable position for your product.

STANDOUT STRATEGIES:

‣ Conduct customer interviews to gather missing insights about how your persona thinks about their pain points, desires, solutions, and the competition.

‣ Partner with your sales team to refine your persona and competitive map. Include them in the research process and incorporate their knowledge of your market.

‣ Choose from a range of other research methods to gather new information from different angles, including customer support listening, social media listening, keyword research, and surveys.

CHAPTER 6

DEFINE YOUR POSITIONING

Andrew, the CEO and founder of a healthcare startup, planned to introduce his product into new cities over the next 12 months. The startup served working professionals who had a range of life challenges and needed more than just health care to stay well, keep their job, and maintain positive relationships. The startup's unique technology platform allowed doctors and providers to work closely together on individualized treatment plans. It also offered a network of remote mental health and career coaches to help with "whole-person" care.

The company's unique approach helped patients significantly improve their health and well-being. But because it was a new concept, it was often hard for Andrew's team to explain what the startup offered. Medical groups and their ideal customers were not familiar with healthcare solutions that offered so many connected services.

"We know that what we offer is special, but we need a better way to explain it to the people who need our services. We want our potential patients to see that we offer a more successful treatment approach than anything else out there," Andrew told me. He needed to create product positioning that would clearly show how their patients would be happier and healthier if they chose the startup's services over other healthcare providers. The growth of the startup depended on it.

Positioning is the sharpest, clearest description of what your product does, who it's for, and why someone should choose your product over all other solutions. It helps your ideal customers understand that your product will generate the best results for their needs. It clarifies the differentiators that make your product uniquely better than alternative solutions. This enables your product to occupy the most favorable "position" against other solutions in your buyer's mind.

As a starting point, answer these questions: What do your ideal customers currently think about your product vs. competitive solutions? Is that how you want your product to be known, and if not, what would you like customers to think instead? In this chapter, you'll learn how to understand your current positioning compared to the other solutions your persona considers. Then, you'll learn techniques to define new positioning and shift your persona's perception of your product.

POSITIONING AND HOW TO SHIFT PERCEPTIONS

Positioning summarizes what makes your product more appealing, desirable, and valuable to your ideal customer than any comparable solution. Thanks to your work in this book so far, you already know the inputs you need to create effective positioning:

✦ **Persona:** Positioning starts with knowing your ideal customer, especially their pains and desired results. This clarifies who your product is for and what they need from a product like yours.

✦ **Category:** A category is the market in which your product
competes. It explains "what" your product is. Your category
includes your direct competitors, but it may not encompass
DIY and indirect competitors.

✦ **Competitive alternatives:** Your competitive map overviews
the alternative solutions your ideal customer considers to
address their problem.

✦ **Differentiators:** Differentiators are your product's unique
benefits and functionality that make it better than
alternative solutions. Your competitive map summarizes
each solution's differentiators.

As a startup, your company will likely have to challenge well-
established competitors to stand out to your customers. When your
persona begins evaluating solutions, they may view these competitors'
products as trusted market leaders in your category. A top priority
is to find a way to describe *your* product's favorable position in the
category too. But before you can define attractive positioning, you
need to identify what criteria influence your persona to select these
leading options. You need to understand how your ideal customers
perceive your product alongside these products.

If most of your competitors fit within a category, you will need to
describe your positioning in the context of that category. Products
within a category tend to offer a common set of benefits and features.
A category also influences customers' expectations about how the
product will work, what outcomes they can expect, and how much
they're willing to pay. As your persona decides which product to buy,
effective positioning and messaging can sway them to select yours.

Sometimes your main competitors don't fit within the same
category. In that case, focus on defining a unique position against

your most important competitors and DIY solutions. Keep an eye on competitive products that emerge, but don't spend time developing insights and messaging around a set of products that your ideal customers don't consider or use. You need to create a favorable contrast with solutions they *do* consider.

Other times, startups want to create a "new category" that better describes how they sit at the intersection of multiple markets. For instance, Andrew's healthcare startup felt that their product was one-of-a-kind because it combined medical, mental health, and career coaching within one platform. These aspects were outside the bounds of a traditional healthcare or medical services category.

But it can take a lot of time and resources for a startup to educate their ideal customers about a completely new category in which they're the only product. Instead, I recommend that early stage startups develop a succinct and compelling way to describe why they're better than the other solutions their persona considers (instead of focusing on category creation).

What makes one product more attractive to your ideal customer than another depends on the criteria they use to make their decision. They'll be drawn to solutions that eliminate their pains, deliver their desired gains, and offer a delightful user experience. But which one is their best choice? To beat your competitors, you need to give customers a framework to evaluate solutions, making your product rise to the top. In the next section, you'll learn how to create a positioning matrix to help you do this.

CREATE A POSITIONING MATRIX

Positioning starts with determining what your ideal customers think about your product vs. competitive solutions today. To do this, you'll create a positioning matrix that captures the status quo. Take your list of top competitors and insights from your competitive map, then pinpoint the top differentiators that draw customers to the leading solutions. Why do your ideal customers choose to buy and use these solutions?

Identify the top two attributes that help your top competitors win. Draw a 2x2 matrix, then list one attribute on the X-axis and the other on the Y-axis. Then, plot your product and your competitors onto this matrix. In the status quo, your ideal customers are drawn to your top competitors' differentiators, so those solutions will be in the upper right quadrant (the most favorable position). When your ideal customers prioritize these characteristics, they will likely choose your competitors. Your product will fall somewhere lower on the map; it's simply less attractive in these dimensions.

STATUS QUO POSITIONING MATRIX: HEALTHCARE STARTUP

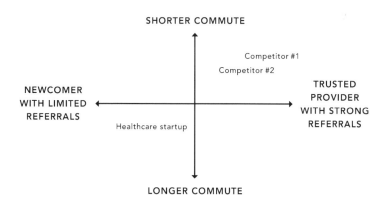

For Andrew's healthcare startup, patients valued a few key things when choosing the market-leading providers. Their top criteria included proximity of providers to their homes and trusted referrals from friends or health care professionals. How did Andrew's startup compare? While the startup's provider network was growing in the cities where they'd launched, they did not have the same volume of providers as market leaders. That meant that many patients had to commute farther to get to their locations. And since the startup's services were relatively unknown, they did not yet have a flywheel of referrals directing patients to their platform.

Looking at this matrix, Andrew knew that these criteria led their ideal customers to a suboptimal solution. This matrix didn't accurately capture the value of their innovative services and platform. Andrew needed to help their ideal customer reconsider what to optimize for when selecting a healthcare network. To address the root cause of their issues, a patient needed not just medical support but also mental health and career coaching services. Their persona needed to work with a set of providers who could share information and create an integrated plan to address their health and wellness needs. While the proximity of providers was important for in-person medical care, it was less important when the patient could meet remotely with their therapist and professional coach.

The healthcare startup wanted to position its product as the best option for the specific type of patient they serve very well. They needed to help their ideal customer use new criteria to evaluate and select their health care providers. Andrew's team had to "flip the matrix" and identify how to create more favorable positioning.

FLIP THE MATRIX TO SHIFT PERCEPTIONS

Positioning helps you find an attractive way to describe exactly what's special about your product vs. competitors in your category and beyond. When you flip the matrix, you create positioning that makes your differentiators shine. It ensures your product appeals to your ideal customers. Using your competitors' current positioning as your anchor point, you'll discover how to describe your product as the obviously more attractive option.

Here are four techniques that will help you flip the matrix and create superior positioning:

+ **New frame:** Suggest new, better criteria for selecting a product in your category.

+ **Opposite attribute:** Stand for a single attribute that's the opposite of your top competitors.

+ **Future cast:** Explain how your product is cutting edge and why your competitors' products are outdated.

+ **Specific segment:** Explain why your product is the best fit for the specific needs of your persona.

Consider each of these positioning techniques to see which one will make your product stand out to your ideal customers so you can flip the matrix

New frame. One path to strong positioning is to introduce new criteria that your ideal customer should use to choose a solution. To position your product using new attributes, you'll need to show customers that the way they currently evaluate solutions is suboptimal. Your persona needs to see that they would get better outcomes if they chose a product based on new criteria. Help them understand the most important things to look for in a product, and show that your product is the best choice in these dimensions.

This is the technique that Andrew's healthcare startup used to position their product as their ideal patient's best option. Their best-fit patients needed to work with a team of providers that collaborated on their care plan. The patients also needed services that extended beyond just health care so they could achieve stability throughout their lives. The startup called these "whole-person services." When placed on the new positioning matrix, the startup's services were clearly the best choice for these customers.

NEW POSITIONING MATRIX: HEALTHCARE STARTUP

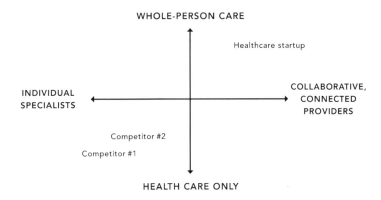

Opposite attribute. There's power in having your product stand for one attribute that contrasts with your competitor's most distinctive strength. What is the top differentiator that your competitor is known for today? Think about the big, bold opposite words you could use to frame your position in the market vs. what your top competitors offer.

When I led marketing at Handshake, a job platform for college students, we used this strategy in several ways to create contrast with a top competitor: LinkedIn. We created pithy "opposite" descriptions that helped our ideal customers, who were college student job seekers, quickly understand why Handshake was the best fit for them. These descriptions included:

✦ Handshake has jobs for college students; LinkedIn has jobs for mid-career professionals.

✦ Handshake helps you find jobs with "no network required;" LinkedIn helps you tap your "network."

✦ Handshake is about your future potential; LinkedIn is about your past resume.

Each of these phrases was a shortcut that we used to explain Handshake's positioning in the job search category. They quickly conveyed why it was the best job platform for students.

Future cast. Show how your product will help customers ride a wave into the future. Your competitor's way of delivering value has been useful to date, but shifts are underway, and your product takes advantage of new, more effective technology. You'll position your product as the cutting-edge way to get better results than legacy products offer. Your product is the right solution for the future, not the past.

I've worked with a range of startups who've launched innovative technologies and used this technique. They position their product as a way to leapfrog old technologies into the future. Examples include:

✦ A construction services platform explains how its state-of-the-art building rendering software enables developers to create more accurate plans, saving time and money on projects.

✦ A medical device company offers a power source that significantly reduces the number of times devices need to be replaced, improving flexibility and quality of life for patients.

✦ A call center training platform uses more sophisticated, tech-enabled education and quality control techniques, improving accuracy and customer experiences on calls with agents they've trained.

Specific segment. Show how your product serves a specific customer segment better than any other competitors. This can be a particularly helpful strategy for early stage startups since delivering an outstanding experience for one specific persona can drive focus in your messaging and help spark word of mouth. Declaring that your product is for a specific type of customer creates immediate contrast with competitors that serve a wider or different audience.

I've worked with several accounting software startups that address the needs of one specific type of business particularly well. Examples include:

✦ One platform focuses on the needs of independent professionals who use software to manage bookings, hourly billing, expenses, and taxes. All of the startup's content, language, and workflows are aimed at these solopreneurs whose businesses focus on hourly clients.

✦ Another startup positions itself as done-for-you accounting services for small business owners who have complex accounting needs and want a turnkey solution. These business owners don't want the responsibility of hiring and managing a freelance accountant and need a predictable bookkeeping process.

✦ At Intuit QuickBooks, we knew our software worked well for a wide range of small businesses. To stand out, we created specific positioning for different types of businesses that had distinctly different needs. For retailers, we talked about the product's strength in managing inventory and paying hourly employees. For professional services providers, we positioned the product as the easiest way to track time and expenses by each client. Differentiated positioning and messaging allowed us to appeal to each segment individually.

Which technique will help you create the best positioning for your startup? Use the template at the end of this chapter to try these four techniques and develop a new positioning matrix for your product. The right technique showcases how your product stands out against top competitors and is the better choice for your ideal customers.

First, decide which differentiators place your product in the upper right of the positioning matrix. Choose two attributes to describe the X and Y axes, then plot your product alongside your competitors. Your product will land in the most favorable position, in the upper right of the positioning matrix. Record your positioning in the *positioning summary* template at the end of this chapter to combine the key insights from your persona, competitive map, and positioning.

CREATE YOUR POSITIONING STATEMENT AND USP

Now you're ready to summarize your positioning and create a unique selling proposition, too. First, create a short positioning statement that describes your product's distinct specialty in your category.

Here's a formula for your short positioning statement:

✦ [Product] is a [category + differentiator] for [ideal customer].

Here are examples of short positioning statements from startups you've met in this book:

✦ Andrew's healthcare startup used: "[Product] is a whole-person healthcare platform for working professionals with complex health needs."

✦ We called Handshake a "career platform for college students" to set it apart from other job platforms that were designed for professionals at later stages in their careers.

✦ We described Thumbtack as a "local services app to check anything off your to-do list" to highlight the breadth of consumer use cases and types of pros on the platform. This contrasted with other players that offered a narrower set of services.

Now create a USP, which is a powerful headline that states how your product uniquely delivers value to your ideal customer. It's your startup's topline message about why your persona should choose your product over the alternatives. A strong USP emphasizes the most desirable outcome your product delivers for your ideal customers as well as your product's top differentiators.

Here's how to craft a unique selling position:

✦ [Product]
✦ is a [category description]
✦ that helps [ideal customer]
✦ with [problem]
✦ achieve [outcome]
✦ through [top differentiators].

Andrew's healthcare startup's USP was:

+ [Product]
+ is a [healthcare platform]
+ that helps [working professionals]
+ with [complex health and career needs]
+ achieve [optimal health and stability]
+ through [connected providers and whole-person services that extend beyond health care].

With your persona and positioning defined, you now have clear signals about how to create effective product messaging. You understand what your ideal customers value about your product. You also understand your product's most attractive differentiators and how to describe your favorable positioning. Now it's time to develop the final "P" that ensures your messaging builds strong affinity with your ideal customers: your brand personality.

STANDOUT STRATEGIES:

‣ Define your product's positioning to summarize how it's different and better than the alternative solutions for your ideal customer.

‣ Build a "status quo" positioning matrix so you understand why your ideal customers choose your top competitors. Then "flip the matrix" to define a new, more favorable position for your product.

‣ Create a compelling USP that's a headline promise about who your product is for, the main outcome it delivers, and its key differentiators.

POSITIONING MATRIX TEMPLATE

STATUS QUO POSITIONING

What are the top attributes that your ideal customer looks for in the solution they select for their pains?

- ✦ 1
- ✦ 2

STATUS QUO POSITIONING MATRIX

Note the attributes (benefits or functionality) on a 2x2 matrix that place your top competitors in the most favorable position. Then, map your top competitors and your product onto the matrix.

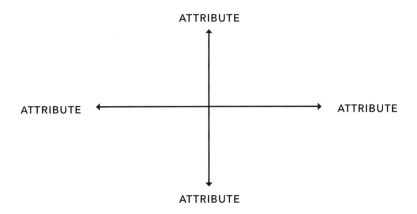

ATTRIBUTE

ATTRIBUTE

ATTRIBUTE

ATTRIBUTE

FLIP THE MATRIX FOR NEW POSITIONING

What attributes place your product in a more favorable position than your competitors? Try these exercises:

Technique	Description
New frame	Suggest new criteria that your ideal customer should use to choose a product, then show that your product is the best along those dimensions.
Opposite attribute	Choose a phrase to describe why your product is the best fit for your ideal customers that is the opposite of the top competitor in your space.

Future cast	Explain why your competitors' old technology is no longer the best choice and why your new technology delivers better results.
Specific segment	Show that your product is purpose-built for your ideal customers and meets their needs better than alternatives made for a different or larger segment.

NEW FRAME

What attributes should your ideal customer prioritize in a solution, which make your product the best choice?

- ✦ 1
- ✦ 2
- ✦ 3

OPPOSITE ATTRIBUTE

What single differentiator contrasts directly with your top competitors in a favorable way?

- ✦ 1
- ✦ 2
- ✦ 3

FUTURE CAST

What differentiators make your product better than legacy solutions and the right choice for the future?

- ✦ 1
- ✦ 2
- ✦ 3

SPECIFIC SEGMENT

What makes your product better for a specific segment of customers than your competitors' solutions?

- ✦ 1
- ✦ 2
- ✦ 3

POSITIONING SUMMARY

PERSONA

Who is your ideal customer? What are their top pains and desires?
(*summarize from your persona template)

- 1
- 2
- 3

CATEGORY

What market categories do you compete in?

- A
- B
- C

COMPETITIVE ALTERNATIVES

What other solutions does your persona consider to solve their pain
points and deliver results? (*pull from your competitive map)

- A
- B
- C

DIFFERENTIATORS

What (1) benefits and (2) functionality make your product different and
better for your persona?

BENEFITS
- 1
- 2
- 3

FUNCTIONALITY
- 1
- 2
- 3

NEW POSITIONING MATRIX

Create a matrix using the attributes that place your product in the most favorable position vs. alternatives. Map each of your top competitors, too.

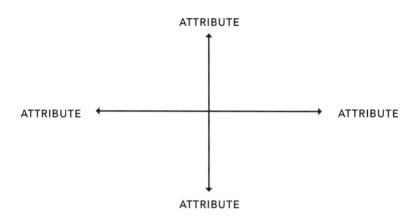

SHORT POSITIONING STATEMENT

Summarize your positioning in a short, differentiating statement.

[Product] is a [category + differentiator] for [ideal customer].

UNIQUE SELLING PROPOSITION

Summarize your headline statement about what your product does, who it's for, and how it's different.

- ✦ [Product]
- ✦ is a [category description]
- ✦ that helps [ideal customer]
- ✦ with [problem]
- ✦ achieve [outcome]
- ✦ through [top differentiators].

CHAPTER 7

CREATE YOUR PERSONALITY

Your brand personality is the final enticing layer you need to create powerful messaging. An appealing brand personality will help your company create a strong connection with your ideal customers. A captivating personality gives your messages a distinctive character and clear point of view. It builds authority, affinity, and trust with your persona. It also helps reinforce the things that differentiate your product.

Brand personality includes three main components:

✦ **Brand attributes:** the unique qualities and character of your brand

✦ **Tone of voice:** how your brand communicates through words, both written and spoken

✦ **Visual brand identity:** the visual elements of your brand (logo, fonts, colors, icons, imagery)

It's vital to define your brand personality before you begin creating messaging and content so that you can communicate consistently. Even across brands, content with the same underlying message can sound and look completely different, depending on the brand's attributes and tone of voice. Your brand personality influences the words you use and the flow, structure, and rhythm of your copy. An intentional personality helps customers anticipate what to expect when you communicate with them, making it easier to build a relationship. As an early stage startup, develop a brand personality that represents your overall company and main product. You can dial up or down elements of your personality and tweak your tone of voice to best communicate with different customer segments.

While this chapter gives you the tools to define your brand attributes and tone of voice, no brand is complete without a visual brand identity. Your brand personality is not crafted from words alone. A visual identity brings your brand attributes to life with a well-designed look that's consistent across your customer touchpoints. With the information captured in your 3 Ps, a design team will have the essential inputs they need to create your visual brand identity. Even better, include a designer in every step of defining your 3 Ps and messaging. They'll add a unique and helpful perspective to the process and will be prepared from the start to create your visual brand identity.

RUN A PERSONALITY WORKSHOP

A great first step to defining your brand personality is through a team workshop. Guide your team through a series of "personality discovery exercises" that draw out what attributes make your brand appealing and distinctive. Pull together a cross-functional team to participate, which could include marketing, sales, product, engineering, design, customer support, and more.

Choose several of the exercises listed below. Some may seem silly on the surface, but they'll spark your team's creativity and will help them recognize your brand's unique qualities. During the workshop, go through these activities one by one, giving participants time to answer the questions and share their ideas. Then cluster words and themes across exercises, recognizing patterns in the way each team member describes your brand. Discuss divergent ideas and which attributes do (and don't) connect with your persona and reflect your brand.

Remind the team that your brand personality needs to be one of a kind and also contrast with top competitors. Everyone needs to understand your product's persona and positioning before joining the workshop. Your personality needs to express the unique way your company communicates with your persona.

CHOOSE YOUR PERSONALITY DISCOVERY EXERCISES

If [brand] were a… Imagine what your brand would be if it existed in a different category (celebrities, cities, animals, types of music, plants, cars, fashion brands, singers, brands, movies). Who or what in these categories best represents your brand? What attributes do they share with your company and product?

Superhero vs. villains. Imagine that your brand is a superhero trying to defeat evil villains. What or who are the villains that your product overcomes? What superpowers does your brand possess to overthrow these villains? What's your superhero's name?

Cocktail party. Imagine your brand is attending a cocktail party and talking to your ideal customers about why they should choose your product. How does your brand look? What does it wear? How does it act? What does it say? Now imagine your brand after it's had a few drinks. What does it say and do now? What attributes get even more exaggerated? Is it funnier, bolder, more direct, or something else?

Anti-brand profile. Imagine a brand that is the exact opposite of your brand. What would your brand never do, act like, or say? If one of your competitor's brands is very different from yours, which characteristics does it embody that are the opposite of your brand? Capture these anti-brand attributes. Then create an on-brand list of attributes that describe your brand.

Brand mood board. Create a mood board of your competitors' brands, placing screenshots on slides or creating a physical collage that captures what you see. Include example headlines, phrases, and content. Show each brand's visual style, including colors, fonts, imagery, and designs. Look across the slides and choose attributes to describe each brand. Now brainstorm what would show up on your new brand mood board, and create a collage of example images, phrases, and designs. Describe the attributes that stand out.

Archetypes. Identifying with a personality archetype is a powerful shortcut to determining your brand personality. As psychoanalyst Carl Jung described, there are universal archetypes that we all instinctively understand and that are immediately recognizable, relatable, and familiar. Each archetype has a top desire that they want to achieve and well-defined personality attributes.

When you identify the archetype that best describes how you provide value and connect with your ideal customers, you'll have a shortlist of attributes that could describe your brand. Using the *brand archetype guide* at the end of this chapter, have your team choose the top one or two archetypes that best express your brand personality. Then note which of those archetype's attributes are a good fit for your startup.

THE TWELVE ARCHETYPES[1]

✦ **The Innocent.** *Desire:* Safety.
Attributes: Trustworthy, Honest, Reliable, Wholesome.

✦ **The Sage.** *Desire:* Understanding.
Attributes: Intelligent, Thoughtful, Analytical, Advisor.

✦ **The Explorer.** *Desire:* Freedom.
Attributes: Independent, Ambitious, Pioneer, Adventurous.

✦ **The Rebel.** *Desire:* Liberation.
Attributes: Risk-taking, Rebellious, Progressive, Brave.

✦ **The Magician.** *Desire:* Power.
Attributes: Intuitive, Clever, Charismatic, Visionary.

✦ **The Hero.** *Desire:* Mastery.
Attributes: Courageous, Strong, Confident, Inspirational.

✦ **The Lover**. *Desire:* Intimacy.
Attributes: Faithful, Passionate, Sensual, Intimate.

✦ **The Jester.** *Desire:* Enjoyment.
Attributes: Humorous, Irreverent, Original, Fun.

1 Margaret Pott Heartwell and Joshua C. Chen, *Archetypes* (New York: HOW Books, 2012).

✦ **The Everyman.** *Desire:* Belonging.
  Attributes: Inviting, Respectful, Fair, Approachable.

✦ **The Caregiver.** *Desire:* Service.
  Attributes: Compassionate, Generous, Empathetic,
  Supportive.

✦ **The Ruler.** *Desire:* Control.
  Attributes: Powerful, Sophisticated, Responsible, Stable.

✦ **The Creator.** *Desire:* Innovation.
  Attributes: Creative, Imaginative, Non-conformist, Unique.

After your workshop, your team will have significant insight into what makes your brand personality appealing and distinctive. The next step is to select your official brand attributes.

SELECT YOUR BRAND ATTRIBUTES

With insights from your workshop, it's time to select three to five brand attributes that describe your brand character. When combined, these attributes encapsulate your brand's singular personality. Revisit the word clusters and themes your team identified during your workshop. These are a strong starting point for your brand attributes. Then have the team go through the *brand attributes worksheet* at the end of this chapter. Each team member will circle words that describe your brand and cross out words that do not align with your personality. You can also print the words on cards, spread them out on a table, and have your team select the attribute cards that describe your brand.

Once again, the next step is to cluster similar words together. Let the team advocate for certain words and clusters and against others. Decide what you can combine and cut. The attributes need to be unique from each other so that your personality has nuance. Once you have a shortlist of words, it's time to make a final decision. Use this checklist to finalize your brand attributes:

+ Is each attribute different? If not, which attributes can be combined or replaced?

+ Are we missing any attributes that capture an appealing aspect of our personality?

+ When combined, do the words accurately describe our brand's personality?

+ Is this personality appealing to our ideal customers?

+ Does this personality create value for our ideal customers?

+ Do these attributes positively emphasize our differentiators?

+ Do these attributes stand out from our top competitors' brand attributes?

+ Do these attributes give us a competitive edge with our ideal customers?

You'll adjust and adapt how you express these attributes to communicate with different audiences. Your underlying personality stays the same, but you'll decide what attributes to amplify or tone down depending on the situation. When you define the right personality attributes, you create an inimitable brand that brings your differentiators to life. Here's a look at the brand attributes that startups from earlier chapters chose and why they're a great fit.

E-commerce security platform: confident, calm, elegant, efficient. Sophia's e-commerce security platform (from chapters 2 and 3) wanted a no-nonsense brand that appealed to their technical, engineering audience. Because the startup dealt with security issues, Sophia wanted their brand to feel like a beacon of calm in a storm. Their platform was purpose-built for the challenges their customers faced, and it was both highly sophisticated and easy to use. The team chose brand attributes that described their platform's sleek, stable presence on an engineering team.
Archetype inspiration: the Ruler

Recruiting platform: bold, empathetic, inspirational, persistent. Lucas's recruiting platform (from chapter 4) wanted to be seen as the no-brainer solution for companies that needed to hire the best talent as soon as possible. The platform needed to convey bold confidence that their recruiters could help high-growth companies hire outstanding people for their open roles. At the same time, they needed a brand that emphasized their focus on candidate experience. The platform gave heads of recruiting access to expert recruiters that shared each company's inspiring mission, motivated candidates to seriously consider their roles, and showed empathy for each candidate's unique needs.
Archetype inspiration: the Hero

Health care startup: supportive, inviting, holistic, effective, stable. Andrew's healthcare startup (from chapter 6) chose brand attributes that showcased how they addressed each patient's comprehensive set of healthcare needs. The startup offered a warm and welcoming program that provided holistic care, and

they wanted their inviting approach to shine through in their personality. They also wanted to contrast with a competitor that came across as their anti-brand: rigid, sterile, and fragmented (but also efficient and credible, which gave them an advantage).
Archetype inspiration: the Caregiver.

Each of these startups was able to establish a clear brand personality, which helped to shape how their customers related to their products and brand. With your attributes defined, fill in the first part of the *brand personality summary* at the end of this chapter. Create a short description of what each attribute means to your brand, then describe your overall brand personality when these attributes combine. After that, it's time to define your brand's tone of voice.

DEFINE YOUR BRAND TONE OF VOICE

Tone of voice refers to your brand's style of communicating with your ideal audience. A consistent tone brings your brand to life through the language and the structure of your communications. What voice appeals to your ideal audience, builds credibility for your product, and matches your brand personality? As a first step, create initial tone guidelines to use as you craft messaging and content in upcoming chapters. You'll refine these over time as you better understand what tone resonates with customers and feels most natural to your brand.

Use these exercises to help you define your tone of voice.

Tone slider. Look through the following characteristics that could describe your tone of voice. Decide where your tone fits along these dimensions and which specific word best describes each aspect of your voice:

How approachable is your tone?	FRIENDLY inviting, casual, relaxed, helpful, conversational, supportive, caring	AUTHORITATIVE professional, proper, smart, formal, serious, sober, deep, informative, technical
How entertaining is your tone?	HUMOROUS funny, silly, playful, upbeat, lighthearted, fresh, comical, hysterical, clever	DRY factual, direct, clear, concise, matter of fact, down-to-earth, straightforward
How passionate is your tone?	EMOTIVE impassioned, enthusiastic, embellished, touching, nostalgic, heartwarming	PROVOCATIVE irreverent, edgy, challenging, unexpected, bold, spicy, moving

Power words. Create a set of power words that you'll use frequently to describe important concepts in your copy and content. These are words that align with your brand personality and will become your brand's unique vocabulary. Repeating this set of power words (while avoiding overkill) helps you create a recognizable and unique tone of voice.

Archetypes. Personality archetypes also give you strong hints about what brand tone will match your personality. Take another look at the *brand archetype guide* at the end of this chapter to see which tone matches the archetype you've incorporated into your brand personality. Select tone descriptions that work for your brand.

Write like this (not like that). Bring your tone of voice to life through examples of copy that use the right tone juxtaposed with two examples that are off in one extreme or the other.

✦ **Write like this:** Show content that is in your tone of voice and describe why it's correct.

✦ **Not like that #1:** Create content that is not in your tone of voice and describe why it's wrong.

✦ **Not like that #2:** Create content that is not in your tone of voice and describe why it's wrong.

Grammar and style rules. Make it clear what specific grammar and style rules you want your team to follow. This could include whether to use sentence or title case in your headings, preferred length of sentences, and more. These intentional decisions make your content more consistent and less confusing to your audience.

Once you fill in the rest of your *brand personality summary*, you'll have an appealing style that your team can infuse into your messaging. And that's not the only thing to celebrate. Congratulations! You've now nailed down your 3 Ps. Defining your personality was the final piece of this puzzle.

Now it's time to move into Part 2: Develop Powerful Product Messaging. You've created the foundation you need to unlock effective messaging that aligns with your persona, positioning, and personality. Move forward with confidence, knowing that you now have the insights to launch messaging that will make your startup stand out and attract, convert, and engage your ideal customers.

STANDOUT STRATEGIES:

‣ Use brand discovery exercises to identify your brand attributes, which define your startup's unique and appealing personality.

‣ Define tone of voice guidelines to ensure you communicate consistently through the words and style in your content.

‣ Brief a design team with your persona and positioning, plus your brand attributes and tone, so they can create a visual brand identity for your brand personality.

BRAND ARCHETYPES GUIDE[2]

ARCHETYPE	BRAND GOAL	BRAND ATTRIBUTES	TONE OF VOICE
GROUP 1: GOAL IS TO SEEK PARADISE			
The Innocent Desire: Safety	Convey strong values, reliability, or simplicity	Trustworthy, Honest, Reliable, Wholesome	Optimistic, Direct, Humble
The Sage Desire: Understanding	Share wisdom and insight as a trusted guide	Intelligent, Thoughtful, Analytical, Advisor	Knowledgeable, Clear, Assured, Guiding
The Explorer Desire: Freedom	Create excitement, offer fulfilling new experiences	Independent, Ambitious, Pioneer, Adventurous	Exciting, Fearless, Daring, Bold
GROUP 2: GOAL IS TO LEAVE A LEGACY			
The Rebel Desire: Liberation	Advocate for change and breaking the old rules	Risk-taking, Rebellious, Progressive, Brave	Honest, Rebellious, Provocative
The Magician Desire: Power	Make dreams come true, transform someone's world	Intuitive, Clever, Charismatic, Visionary	Confident, Informed, Inspiring
The Hero Desire: Mastery	Solve a major problem and improve the world	Courageous, Strong, Confident, Inspirational	Straightforward, Candid, Bold, Inspiring
GROUP 3: GOAL IS TO PURSUE CONNECTION			
The Lover Desire: Intimacy	Help people feel appreciated and loved	Faithful, Passionate, Sensual, Intimate	Warm, Soothing, Appreciative
The Jester Desire: Enjoyment	Help people have a good time	Humorous, Irreverent, Original, Fun	Lighthearted, Funny, Optimistic
The Everyman Desire: Belonging	Be approachable to everyone	Inviting, Respectful, Fair, Approachable	Friendly, Humble, Authentic
GROUP 4: GOAL IS TO PROVIDE STRUCTURE			
The Caregiver Desire: Service	Offer care and protection	Compassionate, Generous, Empathetic, Supportive	Caring, Warm, Reassuring
The Ruler Desire: Control	Create stability and order	Powerful, Sophisticated, Responsible, Stable	Authoritative, Refined, Articulate
The Creator Desire: Innovation	Help people express and create	Creative, Imaginative, Non-conformist, Unique	Inspiring, Daring, Provocative

2 Margaret Pott Heartwell and Joshua C. Chen, *Archetypes* (New York: HOW Books, 2012).

BRAND ATTRIBUTES WORKSHEET

ACTIVE engaged, lively, dynamic, vivacious, energetic	**CAREFUL** thorough, earnest, rigorous, judicious	**DEPENDABLE** sensible, trustworthy, responsible, safe, reliable	**ELEGANT** graceful, stylish, chic, agile, smooth
ADAPTABLE adept, able, skillful, customizable, versatile	**CASUAL** breezy, laid back, earthy, natural, carefree	**DESIRABLE** attractive, alluring, glamorous, hot	**ELITE** leading, pre-eminent, first-rate, fine
ADVENTUROUS audacious, intrepid, pioneering, explorer	**CHARMING** appealing, charismatic, delightful, likable	**DETERMINED** uncompromising, eager, resolute, purposeful	**EMPATHETIC** understanding, feeling, giving, heartfelt, calming
AMBITIOUS daring, industrious, motivated, driven	**CLASSIC** excellent, traditional, timeless, unforgettable	**DIGNIFIED** noble, grand, majestic, elevated, regal	**ENTERTAINING** amusing, enjoyable, engaging, pleasurable
APPROACHABLE convenient, accessible, receptive, easygoing	**CLEAR** specific, unmistakable, transparent, precise	**DILIGENT** hard-working, tireless, meticulous, rigorous	**ENTREPRENEURIAL** enterprising, go-getter, innovative, experimental
ASPIRATIONAL magnetic, inspiring, dreamy, captivating	**COMFORTABLE** easy, cozy, relaxed, satisfying, calming	**DISCRETE** tactful, diplomatic, cautious, low-key	**ETHICAL** just, moral, virtuous, reputable
AUTHORITATIVE masterful, factual, decisive, assertive	**COMPASSIONATE** empathetic, caring, comforting, soothing	**DISTINCTIVE** exceptional, outstanding, extraordinary, famed	**EXCITING** thrilling, exhilarating, breathtaking
BALANCED fair, unbiased, open-minded, harmonious	**CONFIDENT** assured, feisty, secure, unshakeable	**DISTINGUISHED** acclaimed, prestigious, renowned, esteemed	**EXPERT** skilled, accomplished, authoritative, talented
BEAUTIFUL attractive, lovely, gorgeous, splendid	**CONSISTENT** predictable, enduring, unyielding, certain	**EAGER** enthusiastic, hungry, excited, stoked	**FASCINATING** captivating, intriguing, enchanting
BRAVE courageous, bold, fearless, gutsy	**CREATIVE** visionary, original, ingenious, imaginative	**ECONOMICAL** prudent, affordable, saving, frugal	**FOCUSED** intent, obsessed, committed, attentive
CALM patient, serene, tranquil, peaceful, gentle	**CURIOUS** remarkable, inquisitive, mysterious, interested	**EDGY** provocative, forerunner, thought-provoking	**FRESH** novel, forward, refreshing, crisp, saucy

BRAND ATTRIBUTES WORKSHEET

FRIENDLY pleasant, nice, gracious, amicable, kind	**INSPIRATIONAL** motivating, energizing, uplifting, influential	**PASSIONATE** expressive, fervent, fiery, spirited, vigilant	**SIMPLE** effortless, uncomplicated, quick, easy
FUN playful, festive, merry, cheeky	**INTELLIGENT** smart, bright, sharp, quick, brainy	**PERSISTENT** firm, steady, tenacious, unwavering	**SPONTANEOUS** impromptu, instinctive, improvised, automatic
GENIUS maven, virtuoso, brilliant, wizard	**INTIMATE** private, personal, familiar, secret	**POLISHED** refined, sophisticated, glossy, sleek	**STRATEGIC** planned, principled, intentional, forward
GREEN eco-friendly, sustainable, conservationist, organic	**INVITING** welcoming, appealing, hospitable, genial	**POWERFUL** persuasive, intense, impressive, forceful	**STRONG** vigorous, tough, robust, mighty, rugged
HAPPY joyful, cheerful, sunny, lighthearted, content	**KNOWLEDGEABLE** experienced, informed, sage, seasoned	**PRACTICAL** functional, reasonable, pragmatic, useful	**SUPPORTIVE** helpful, celebratory, comforting, affirming
HOMEGROWN native, local, regional, homemade	**LOGICAL** analytical, objective, rational, scientific	**PRODUCTIVE** prolific, effective, efficient, valuable	**THOUGHTFUL** generous, respectful, considerate, mindful
HONEST sincere, genuine, frank, candid, open, credible	**LUXURIOUS** deluxe, extravagant, lavish, upscale	**PROFESSIONAL** experienced, specialized, technical, trained	**TRAILBLAZER** pioneer, cutting-edge, author, architect
HUMOROUS funny, witty, hilarious, comical, hysterical	**MODERN** contemporary, current, state-of-the-art, new	**QUIRKY** peculiar, weird, wacky, offbeat, wild, alternative	**UNIQUE** rare, unparalleled, exotic, one-of-a-kind
INDEPENDENT unconventional, individual, nonconformist	**NURTURING** cultivating, guiding, fostering, protective	**RESILIENT** flexible, stable, durable, long-lasting	**VERSATILE** customizable, bespoke, flexible, variable
INFORMAL easygoing, leisurely, straightforward, simple	**OPTIMISTIC** encouraging, hopeful, positive, reassuring	**RESOURCEFUL** savvy, capable, gifted, crafty	**VIGOROUS** hearty, spirited, youthful, vivacious, powerhouse
INSIGHTFUL perceptive, wise, clever, intuitive, aware	**ORGANIZED** systematic, disciplined, structured, methodical	**ROMANTIC** tender, loving, sexy, affectionate, sweet	**WHIMSICAL** outlandish, eccentric, singular, fantastical

PERSONALITY SUMMARY

BRAND ATTRIBUTES

List your brand attributes and describe their meaning to your ideal customers and your company.

ATTRIBUTE	MEANING
Attribute #1	Description
Attribute #2	Description
Attribute #3	Description
Attribute #4	Description
Attribute #5	Description

BRAND CHARACTER

Describe your brand character, which combines your brand attributes into a personality.

- A
- B
- C

BRAND TONE OF VOICE

What words best describe the tone of voice you use to communicate with your audience?

- A
- B
- C

POWER WORDS

What are the preferred words and phrases that your team uses in content?

+ 1
+ 2
+ 3
+ 4
+ 5

WRITE LIKE THIS (NOT THAT)

Give examples of content that embody your tone of voice.

+ **Write like this:** Show content in your ideal tone of voice and describe why this is correct.

+ **Not like that (Extreme #1):** Show content that is not in your tone of voice and describe why.

+ **Not like that (Extreme #2):** Show content that is not in your tone of voice and describe why.

PART 2

DEVELOP POWERFUL PRODUCT MESSAGING

CHAPTER 8

DEVELOP STRONG VALUE PROPOSITIONS

This is a pivotal moment. You have all the elements you need to create powerful product messaging. You've already developed a strong USP through your positioning work. Now, you'll learn the importance of a product messaging framework and how to develop the next essential element: value propositions.

Value propositions (value props, for short) are concise, punchy statements about your product's top benefits. Value props are the most important things your ideal audience needs to understand about your product to realize it's their best fit. Your value props need to be enticing and memorable. They also need to be repeatable, so that you and your team can reiterate them across sales pitches, marketing collateral, and content. Soon we'll discuss the characteristics of effective value propositions and a process to develop them.

First, let's look at the structure and role of a messaging framework, where you'll capture all the pieces of your messaging strategy.

CREATE A PRODUCT MESSAGING FRAMEWORK

A product messaging framework summarizes the most compelling messages you'll use to attract, convert, and engage your ideal customers. This way, you can equip your team with a source-of-truth summary that guides the messaging they use across customer touchpoints. As you know from part 1 of this book, the 3 Ps provide the critical insights you need to craft distinctive messaging for each of your personas. This means that each key member of your buying committee, if you're a B2B startup, will encounter messages intentionally created for them. If you're a B2C startup, each unique customer segment will have its own framework.

An effective product messaging framework includes three main components:

+ **Promise:** Your USP succinctly describes who your product is for, what outcome you promise, and how your product is differentiated. You created a USP for your primary persona in chapter 6.

+ **Benefits:** Next you'll create three value proposition statements that describe the most desirable benefits your product delivers for your ideal customers. These are the main messages you want your persona to remember about your product because they highlight its differentiated value.

+ **Proof:** Finally, you need to share evidence to validate that your product can deliver these results. Proof points that build credibility for your product and company include features, social proof, endorsements, data, and information. You'll learn all about proof points in chapter 9.

Here's how each of these components fits together in a messaging framework. You'll find a *product messaging framework* template at the end of this chapter for you to fill in.

PRODUCT MESSAGING FRAMEWORK

PRODUCT NAME			
PERSONA DESCRIPTION			
UNIQUE SELLING PROPOSITION			
Benefit	Benefit #1	Benefit #2	Benefit #3
Value Prop	Value Prop #1	Value Prop #2	Value Prop #3
Functionality	Features How it works	Features How it works	Features How it works
Social Proof	Customer stories Case studies Endorsements Exec platform	Customer stories Case studies Endorsements Exec platform	Customer stories Case studies Endorsements Exec platform
Data & Information	Data FAQs Guides	Data FAQs Guides	Data FAQs Guides

This is the messaging framework you'll fill in for each of your personas. But first, let's dig into how to create effective value propositions.

LEARN THE ROLE OF EFFECTIVE VALUE PROPS

Thanks to your 3 Ps, you already have clarity around what your ideal customers value and what differentiates your product from the competition. Now you need to craft value propositions that share strong claims about the benefits of using your product. These benefits reinforce how your product achieves the outcome you promised in your USP, and what makes your product both desirable and unique. Your value props also provide a structure that communicates the value of your key features. They create a consistent, comprehensive way to talk about your product's advantages.

When your ideal customer compares your value props to your competitors', it will be obvious why your product is a better fit for their needs. As a test, if you copied and pasted your value props onto a top competitor's website and they'd accurately explain this competitor's product, you need to rework them. Your value props, infused with your product's unique value and your personality, should showcase how your solution is truly one of a kind.

You'll create three value props for your messaging frameworks. It's easier for your ideal customers to remember things in sets of three, and these are the messages you'll emphasize through a range of interactions with them. Limiting your list to three key messages also forces you to select your most appealing benefits.

Think of value props as three pillars or three legs of a stool, supporting your USP. Each "leg" needs to work hard on its own, and together they need to fully support and deliver your USP's big promise. If you cut one, you'd leave out a benefit that is particularly enticing to your ideal customer, and your product may seem too similar to your competitors' solutions. Make sure that each value prop is different and compelling.

To sharpen and simplify your value props, first choose one word that explains the key benefit you want to convey. Add that to the "benefit" line in your messaging framework. Then craft a value proposition sentence that explains that benefit to your persona. Don't worry about polishing the wording yet. You'll refine the copy and add your brand personality to the messaging as a final step in creating your messaging framework.

How can you craft compelling value props? The checklist below describes eight characteristics to use as a guide.

FOLLOW THIS VALUE PROPOSITIONS CHECKLIST

Your value propositions need to convey your product's value in just a few phrases. As you craft your value props, follow these guidelines to make them as strong as possible. You'll also find this *value propositions checklist* summarized at the end of this chapter.

Results-oriented. Strong value props speak to the benefits and results your product delivers. Start each value prop statement in one of the following ways:

✦ **Action verb:** Start with an action verb to convey what the product does or delivers.
Examples: save, grow, increase, promote, achieve, create, run, gain, boost, reduce

✦ **Descriptor:** Start with either an adjective or adverb that makes a claim about your product.
Examples: easily, simply, smart, reliable, comprehensive, powerful, proactive, most, best, least, strongest

Feature-friendly. Each of your most important features will help deliver the benefits captured in your value props. For instance, the key features in your product will help your customers achieve results like "save time," "reduce expenses," or "boost sales." As you develop value props, list the key features that support each one. Make sure you're not leaving out any important features, which could mean you're overlooking one of the key gains your product delivers.

Desirable. Your value props need to attract and appeal to your ideal customers. You understand what your persona desires, so make sure that your value props address the top functional, emotional, and social gains they want to achieve.

Differentiated. Value props need to help you stand out from the competition and showcase your product's differentiated benefits. Aim for at least two of your value props to be unique to your product. In other words, you need to create value props that you wouldn't find listed on your competitor's website or highlighted in their sales pitch.

Durable. Make sure your value props represent the most significant benefits that your product will offer for the next year or more. Think about how your product will evolve over the next several quarters. Consider what major features you'll launch and the benefits they'll create. Then check whether your value props convey the value of these features, too.

Defensible. Select value props that create a competitive moat and are difficult for competitors to replicate. You want your value props to have longevity, so your product becomes known for these distinctive strengths over the long term.

Distinct. Ensure that your value props don't overlap with each other and are not repetitive. Your messaging framework only includes three, so get the most out of each one and explain a separate compelling benefit. This will help you maximize the value you communicate in your messaging.

Comprehensive. When you read through all your value props together, they need to create a complete picture of the most valuable benefits that your product offers. Even with only three pithy phrases, you can capture the most enticing results that your customer can expect from your product.

With all of these aspects of effective value props in mind, let's talk about how to create them for your product.

CREATE STRONG VALUE PROPOSITIONS

Running a value props workshop is a great way to explore and narrow in on what benefit statements to use. Remember that your value props need to appeal to a specific persona, so you'll do this exercise several times if you have multiple personas. You'll create value props that are customized for each persona's needs to increase connection and conversion with each audience.

To participate in the workshop, team members need to be grounded in your startup's persona, competitive map, positioning, and personality. Be sure they understand the value proposition checklist too. Start by going broad, asking everyone to come up with five to eight potential benefits and value prop phrases. Then have everyone share their list and cluster similar benefits together. Begin to narrow in on your three most powerful value props. Use the checklist to verify that each statement is effective and that, together, this set of value props is the winning combination.

The startups you met in part 1 of this book used this approach to develop their value props. Their statements are results-oriented, create a framework to describe key features, and highlight different benefits. Here's a longer list of phrases that each startup considered before they narrowed down to three compelling value props.

E-COMMERCE SECURITY SOFTWARE

FOUNDER: SOPHIA *Persona: engineering director*

- ✦ **Proactive detection:** Never miss a threat with continuous monitoring.
- ✦ **Fast implementation:** Save time and effort when you implement this turnkey solution.
- ✦ **Alerts:** Immediate detection when a breach occurs so you save customers and revenue.
- ✦ **Cutting-edge:** Latest threat monitoring technology that's better than in-house expertise.
- ✦ **No downtime:** Deliver the best customer experience with no downtime or disruption.

FREELANCE RECRUITING MARKETPLACE

FOUNDER: LUCAS *Persona: head of recruiting*

- ✦ **Specialists:** Access the exact recruiter you need to hire the right person for each role.
- ✦ **Savings:** Eliminate fixed costs as your recruiting needs scale up and down.
- ✦ **Tracking:** Gain complete visibility into each candidate's progress and understand your pipeline.
- ✦ **Flexibility:** Switch recruiters anytime to ensure you have the best match.
- ✦ **Close rates:** Close candidates faster when you hire specialized recruiters with strong networks.

HEALTHCARE PLATFORM

FOUNDER: ANDREW *Persona: working professional with complex wellness needs*

- ✦ **Comprehensive:** Treatment for every aspect of your health and lifestyle so you get sustainable results.
- ✦ **Inviting:** Inviting and welcoming services so you feel comfortable each step of the way.
- ✦ **Affordable:** Affordable, flexible payments that won't let budget stand in your way.
- ✦ **Holistic:** Holistic care from providers who partner to help with all aspects of your health.
- ✦ **Proven:** Proven results through a program adapted exactly to your needs.

What happens after you decide on your three value props? For now, add them to your product messaging framework so you have a strong messaging draft. Some startup leaders feel confident about their statements right away and are ready to launch them throughout their marketing and sales collateral. Other leaders want to test and refine their value props before updating customer touchpoints. I'd encourage you to do some research and testing before you lock them in, and you'll find a range of ways to do this in chapter 10.

You can also revisit the USP that you developed in chapter 6 as part of your positioning work. Your USP incorporates your top differentiators and mentions your top benefits, too. Refine your USP if you've come up with new insights and smarter benefits in the process of developing your value props.

The next step in developing your messaging framework is to create proof points that validate your benefit claims. You'll learn about a toolbox of powerful proof points in the next chapter.

STANDOUT STRATEGIES:

› Develop a messaging framework that includes a strong USP, value propositions, and proof points for each of your personas so you have a go-to set of effective messages.

› Create three value props that describe the most important benefits your product delivers and that make your product stand out to your ideal customers.

› Use the value propositions checklist to develop effective value propositions that are results-oriented, feature-friendly, desirable, differentiated, durable, defensible, distinct, and comprehensive.

PRODUCT MESSAGING FRAMEWORK

PRODUCT NAME

Product name

PERSONA

Description of your ideal customer
- 1
- 2
- 3

UNIQUE SELLING PROPOSITION

[Product] is a [category description] that helps [ideal customer] with [problem] achieve [outcome] through [top differentiators].

VALUE PROP #1

Benefit:

Value Proposition:
- 1
- 2
- 3

Functionality: Features / How it works
- 1
- 2
- 3

Social Proof:
Customer stories / Case studies / Endorsements / Executive platform
- 1
- 2
- 3

Data & Information: Data / FAQs / Guides
- 1
- 2
- 3

VALUE PROP #2

Benefit:

Value Proposition:
   ✦ 1
   ✦ 2
   ✦ 3

Functionality: Features / How it works
   ✦ 1
   ✦ 2
   ✦ 3

Social Proof:
Customer stories / Case studies / Endorsements / Executive platform
   ✦ 1
   ✦ 2
   ✦ 3

Data & Information: Data / FAQs / Guides
   ✦ 1
   ✦ 2
   ✦ 3

VALUE PROP #3

Benefit:

Value Proposition:
   ✦ 1
   ✦ 2
   ✦ 3

Functionality: Features / How it works
   ✦ 1
   ✦ 2
   ✦ 3

Social Proof:
Customer stories / Case studies / Endorsements / Executive platform
   ✦ 1
   ✦ 2
   ✦ 3

Data & Information: Data / FAQs / Guides
   ✦ 1
   ✦ 2
   ✦ 3

VALUE PROPOSITION CHECKLIST

Review each of your value propositions to make sure they meet these eight criteria.

CRITERIA	DESCRIPTION
Results-oriented	Starts with an action verb or descriptor
Feature-friendly	Creates three groups of features that deliver each benefit
Desirable	Conveys the most important benefits your product offers
Differentiated	Shows how your product is different and better than the competitors
Durable	Encapsulates top benefits as you release features over the next 12+ months
Defensible	Notes a distinctive strength that sets you apart from competitors over the long run
Distinct	Describes three significantly different benefits
Comprehensive	Describes your product's value holistically

CHAPTER 9

SUPPORT WITH PROOF POINTS

The next critical part of your product messaging framework is to prove that your product will deliver the exciting results you promise. You'll spark interest and desire for your product with your USP and value propositions. Proof points validate your product's impact and build trust. They give your ideal customer the confidence they need to choose your product over all the others.

You need to identify what "reasons to believe" resonate most with your ideal customer. The three main types of proof points include:

✦ **Functionality:** The features and unique user experience that deliver your product's benefits.

✦ **Social proof:** User stories and external endorsements that confirm your product's effectiveness.

✦ **Data and information:** Metrics and content that verify how your product delivers results.

In your messaging framework, you'll add a strong list of these proof points to support each value proposition. Proof points help you connect both emotionally and logically with your ideal customer. They work to overcome your persona's "blockers" and serve as strong "motivators" too (you captured these in your persona in chapter 3). The list of proof points below is a toolkit of options to substantiate the results your product delivers for customers.

You may wonder, *What proof points do I choose?* As you work through this chapter, consider which types of proof points are most trustworthy and motivating to your persona. What objections and questions does your persona have, and what information can overcome them? What kinds of data and stories inspire your ideal customer? Focus on generating the type of proof points your persona will respect most, and don't waste your time chasing information that isn't engaging or useful for your audience. Here's a breakdown of the types of proof points you can create.

PROOF POINTS OVERVIEW

TYPE	PROOF POINT	DESCRIPTION
Functionality	Features	Product functionality that produces results and benefits
	How it works	Framework that overviews how your product operates
Social Proof	Customer stories	Testimonials sharing customers' experiences and results
	Case studies	Content showcasing how customers achieved positive results
	Endorsements	Press, awards, and third-party validation of your product
	Executive platform	Thought leadership and credibility of company leaders

Data and Information	Data	Metrics that validate your benefits and results
	Resources / Guides	Value-add content that helps customers use your product
	FAQs	Answers to questions that overcome common objections

We'll walk through each type, so you can decide what's most compelling for your ideal customers and the best for your messaging framework.

HIGHLIGHT FUNCTIONALITY THAT DRIVES RESULTS

Highlight the key product features that support each value prop as your first set of proof points. This will build your ideal customer's confidence that your product can do the work to deliver the results you promise. A compelling "how it works" overview will showcase the unique way your product solves your customer's challenges. Emphasize your unique user experience and important functionality to build trust.

Features. Describe the set of features that deliver each of your top benefits. List these features under the value prop they support. As you release new features, you can show customers how the new functionality helps your product deliver even better results related to that value prop. This entices them to try and actively use the new capabilities in your product.

How it works. Create an easy-to-understand framework that overviews the steps to use your product. This overview offers a clear, digestible way to describe your unique method for delivering results. It creates a memorable summary of your product's approach and systems. It also previews the user experience and differentiates your product from competitors. A clear "how it works" overview helps a prospect anticipate what to expect when they start to use your product. It highlights the actions new customers need to take to get results. A product experience that is easier to use, faster, more comprehensive, more delightful, or more tailored to your persona can give your product an edge.

Sophia's e-commerce security startup (that you met in chapters 2 and 3) needed a compelling way to show engineering directors how their software works. Their persona wanted a comprehensive, low-effort way to monitor and quickly take action on any security threats that affected their shopping site. Sophia and her team created an overview of the "five-step system" that their software used to monitor, diagnose, alert, repair, and strengthen after threats. The startup also highlighted features of their unique monitoring technology that delivered the results in each step. This at-a-glance overview of the platform built the engineering director's confidence that the software managed everything they needed to keep the site safe.

USE SOCIAL PROOF TO BUILD CONFIDENCE

One of the most powerful types of proof points is social proof, which relies on the positive opinions of customers and trusted influencers to build confidence with your ideal customers. Share stories of actual customers' successes throughout your marketing so your ideal customer can picture themselves getting the same great outcomes. Showcase third-party endorsements like media coverage, awards, and influencer mentions to create instant credibility. Another authority-builder is to establish your founder and executives as thought leaders in your industry, increasing conviction that your team knows how to deliver results.

Customer stories. Stories, feedback, and testimonials from customers about why they love your product can be one of the best ways to build trust. Customer quotes, reviews, and user-generated content highlight the positive results that relatable customers achieved with your product. Users share the transformation they experienced and recommend why your product is the right choice. Customers can explain how approachable, comprehensive, user-friendly, or useful your product is, which helps your other ideal customers see themselves achieving the same results.

Case studies. While customer stories share customers' experiences in their own words, a case study is an example you create to showcase how a customer achieved outstanding results. Case studies explain your customer's starting point, their experience using your product, and their success, so your ideal audience can picture themselves in the same situation with similar results. You can also create a range of case studies that appeal to each of your specific personas, increasing the stories' relevance and relatability.

Endorsements. Many types of third-party endorsements build confidence in the results your product can deliver. Endorsements include awards, press coverage, quotes from respected leaders or associations, and more. When a trusted source validates that your product is effective and your company is great to work with, your ideal customer will take notice. Place snippets from articles, comments from influencers, and icons of awards in your marketing collateral to ensure your ideal customers notice these endorsements.

Executive platform. Company executives can also build your product's credibility through their thought leadership and positive reputation. Leaders earn social proof when they speak on influential platforms, share thoughtful content, and establish themselves in their industry. Sometimes your leaders' successful experiences at past companies will create a halo effect and help build trust in your company's ability to deliver results.

The e-commerce security platform used social proof to demonstrate to engineering directors that their product was effective. Sophia's startup shared multiple customer testimonials about the positive impact the security platform had on their businesses. These stories were particularly helpful for their primary buyer, the engineering director, to share with their CEO, the final decision maker, who wanted to see that other reputable shopping sites trusted this product. A strong set of customer stories built credibility throughout the sales process.

Sophia also had years of experience working at the exact types of companies her product served. Her expert perspective and the thought leadership content she shared made the startup and its product more trustworthy. Sophia guested on podcasts and garnered press coverage that the team could repurpose as proof points throughout their marketing. Her reputation and executive platform helped the team get traction with customers, too.

OFFER DATA AND INFORMATION THAT PROVES EFFECTIVENESS

Another effective way to build your persona's confidence is through data and information about your product's impact. Highlight key statistics and metrics that prove users' success with the product.

Share "how-to" content (like quick start guides) to build your persona's confidence that they can easily learn how to use your product. You can also address common questions and objections directly through FAQs.

Data. Facts, metrics, and statistics can demonstrate the results your product delivers. Data points can prove useful facts, like time saved, revenue generated, customers reached, and other measurable outcomes. Consider what data best legitimizes your claims and the outcome you promise in your USP.

Resources and guides. How-to content that helps customers use your product will also build your persona's confidence. Don't save all of your resources and guides for the onboarding process. Open them up and offer them to prospective customers so they can preview the product, increasing your persona's faith that they can successfully achieve the outcomes they need most. These resources can include articles, videos, podcasts, shortcuts, tips, or any other guide that shows your ideal customers how to get results from your product.

FAQs. Proactively answer your ideal customer's common questions and concerns. Weave answers throughout your content and publish a set of your ideal customers' frequently asked questions that are holding them back from choosing your product. Anticipate must-know information, bypass hesitations, and address key concerns head-on.

Sophia's team knew that engineering directors were very interested in data that proved the security platform's results. Their persona wanted to see quantifiable outcomes that other companies experienced when using the software. The startup shared specific case studies with data about their customers' uptime, threats identified and eliminated, and time to restore the site after a breach occurred. The startup also shared metrics on how these results compared to industry benchmarks.

The engineering directors also wanted to make sure their teams could easily implement, learn, and use the platform. To reduce their engineering teams' time spent on security monitoring and maintenance, the startup offered step-by-step videos that they called the "Security Academy." The course taught all of the key aspects of the product to make learning how to use the security software as fast and straightforward as possible.

Once you determine which proof points will be most influential for your ideal customer, add them to the product messaging framework you started developing in chapter 8. When you begin part 3 of this book, you'll be ready to update your marketing touchpoints with all of these new messaging elements.

But first, you'll need to see how customers respond to your new messages in the real world. Now that you have a complete draft of your messaging, it's time to get customer feedback. The next chapter shows you ways to test your messages, see what drives customer action, and rapidly refine your messaging.

STANDOUT STRATEGIES:

▸ Create proof points that build trust and confidence among your ideal customers that your product can deliver the benefits you promise.

▸ Highlight product features and create an overview of how your product works to build customers' confidence that your product delivers results.

▸ Showcase ample social proof, data, and information that add credibility and validate your value props. Add all these points to your messaging framework to weave into your marketing.

CHAPTER 10

TEST YOUR MESSAGES

At this stage, most founders are thinking, *How do we know that these messages will actually work?* The next step is to make sure they attract, convert, and engage customers. It's important to make smart refinements. To do that, you'll gather customer feedback and run tests to see how your new messages perform when they're live.

A startup marketplace for caterers needed to update their messaging to entice a new segment of customers to try their service. Their CEO and cofounder, William, and his team had identified many use cases for catering, including family meal delivery, office meals, large events, and smaller celebrations. The startup had successfully launched and gotten traction with individuals who needed catering for family meals at their homes and the personal events they hosted. Now, the startup wanted to break into catering for offices and corporate events. "Our growth depends on finding messages that will cut through and drive orders from this new set of customers," William told me. His team did the work to develop a new messaging framework, then we created a plan to interview customers and test the messages through ads, landing pages, and emails.

There are many ways to test messages before you go all in on updating your marketing and sales collateral. I suggest that you plan your research in two stages. First, you'll refine messages based on customer input, then you'll run tests to understand actual customer behavior.

✦ **Messaging validation:** Get initial feedback on your messaging framework, refine the wording, and narrow down to the most promising messages to test with customers in real scenarios.

✦ **Customer testing:** Roll out your messaging in controlled tests to measure actual customer engagement and conversion within key channels.

In the next sections, I'll share some of the most approachable and speedy methods you can use for both messaging validation and customer testing. Let's dive in.

GET CUSTOMER INPUT TO VALIDATE YOUR MESSAGES

The first step is to gather customer input to strengthen and polish your messaging framework. A round of research will help you solidify these messages based on reactions from your ideal customers. You've already captured a strong draft of your USP, value propositions, and proof points from your work in the past few chapters. If you're still considering several versions of your messages, you can get customer feedback on which ones are the most enticing. You can also listen to the questions customers ask and hear how they repeat back the messages in their own words. This will help you incorporate the actual language your ideal customers use. You'll use these inputs to refine your messaging framework.

There are a few helpful ways to get customer feedback on your messaging:

Customer interviews. Run interviews and share your messaging concepts with both current and potential customers. You can ask the interviewee to rank or rate different versions of your USP and value props to see which ones are most appealing and useful. You can also share different combinations of value props and proof points to see what people find most credible. After the conversations, look at patterns from the interviews and narrow down your messages to a few that you'll test in the next stage.

After going through the 3 Ps process and developing their USP, value props, and proof points, William's team was ready to get feedback from their persona. They'd already talked to a range of people in charge of ordering food for office meals during their research phase (refer to chapter 5). Now it was time to get reactions from this new segment of ideal customers, which included executive assistants, office managers, and corporate event planners. The value props the team developed for this audience were significantly different from the ones they were using to attract families to the catering marketplace. William wanted input to get reactions from this new group.

William and his team found that some of their messages were spot on, and others missed the mark. After talking with office managers, the startup realized they needed to add stronger messaging around the ease of customizing orders. Their persona emphasized that this functionality was crucial given the range of dietary needs and food preferences they had to balance on their teams. This was not a value prop that the startup had originally landed on, but William's team realized it was a key differentiator. So they created a new value prop: "Easily customize meals for every member of your team." William's team also listened to how their ideal customers described their needs and desired results, then they infused these exact words into their value props and proof points.

William's team also considered other research techniques:

Survey. Gather customer input via a survey where you ask participants to rate, rank, or give feedback on your different messages. Surveys allow you to rapidly collect information from a larger quantity and broader group of people. Keep the questions uncomplicated and the survey short to increase response rates and improve data quality. Then analyze the results to see what messages rise to the top.

Sales pitch test. Create different variations of your messaging to test during sales conversations. You can include a few different slides in your sales deck or create an updated one-pager that weaves in your new messages. The sales team can note differences in prospects' reactions, questions, and conversion rates after each conversation. The goal of this research is to get a pulse check on how well new messages work, but not overhaul the sales script yet.

Social media input. Run a quick poll, ask an engaging question, or post messaging options and ask for comments. Because this type of test plays out in public, you need to think carefully about what you share. But if you have an engaged community of prospects and customers on a social media platform, this can be a helpful way to quickly get reactions.

RUN MESSAGING TESTS TO SEE WHAT CONVERTS

After your initial wave of research, it's time to see how your persona behaves when they encounter these new messages in your marketing. Rather than just listening to what people have to say about your messages, you'll roll out the messaging in select marketing channels and measure what customers do in response.

As you test new messages in ads, landing pages, emails, and other channels, you'll measure actual user behavior. Decide in advance which metrics you want to track—changes in customer engagement, click-through rates, open rates, conversion rates, time on the page, or something else—to see which messages drive the most engagement. Determine the structure and duration of your tests according to what you want to learn.

There are a few important things to keep in mind as you design your messaging tests:

+ **Input from your persona is what matters:** Be sure to test engagement from your ideal audience, not people who aren't the customers you're trying to attract and convert. People who fit your persona are the filter for all of your messaging decisions.

+ **Think ahead about the length of the tests:** The more quickly you can drive a volume of traffic into your test, the sooner you'll get a signal. Be realistic about how long you'll need to run each test and the resources it will require, such as how many emails to send or your ad budget.

+ **Test divergent versions of your messages:** The messages you test need to be strikingly different from each other for you to detect significant differences in customer reactions. If you test messages that only have subtle differences, it will leave you unsure about which variant influenced behavior.

One more important note: No matter what the results of the tests tell you, you'll need to use your judgment about which messages to roll out in your marketing. New messaging may not immediately beat your current messaging in a test, even if it contains stronger components. Marketing and sales teams make many ongoing tweaks to optimize messaging once it's in the wild and they see what converts customers.

Even if your tests show flat or slightly negative conversion, you're still likely on the right path. Making a bold move to create messaging that better addresses the needs of your persona and more clearly differentiates your product will win over time. These tests will inform revisions before you update your website, sales, and marketing collateral more broadly.

Consider this list of options as you're planning your tests:

Landing page test. Develop landing pages with divergent messages to see which one drives the most engagement. Measure time on page and clicks to sign up, request a demo, or download content. You can test new versions of your home page or standalone landing pages. Direct traffic from email or ads to different variants and then measure engagement.

Digital ad test. Rapidly test reactions to different messages through social media ads or search engine ads targeted at your ideal customers. You'll be able to see what headlines catch your ideal customers' attention and drive clicks (you'll learn more about hooks in chapter 16). It's easier to test and optimize a wide variety of messages through ads than through any of the other testing types.

Email subject line test. Test open rates and click-through rates on emails with different subject lines (but with the same content in the email). This is another good way to test hooks and the phrasing of your USP, value props, and proof points to see what captures attention and drives your persona to open the email.

Email content test. Test engagement with emails that contain different content (keeping subject lines the same) to understand which value props and proof points resonate in the body of the email. You could test a single email or a multi-email series that uses divergent messaging. You'll want to measure clicks on the call to action, which could be to view content, watch a video, request a call, or something else relevant to your sales process.

When William's catering marketplace wanted to see what messages attracted and converted their ideal office manager persona, they launched a series of tests over two weeks. First, the team worked with an agency to test social media ads with a wide range of copy and creative concepts. They drove traffic to landing pages that were specifically designed to introduce their office catering options to their new audience. During this test, the company was able to see exactly what ads drove the most clicks. They also learned that the landing page emphasizing the "range of choices and quality of food" on the platform drove more sign-ups than a landing page that talked about the "ease of ordering and saving team preferences."

With these insights, William felt clearer about their strongest messages and more confident about their go-to-market plans for office catering customers. The team continued to test the messages in other channels, too, including via email subject lines and content experiments. After these tests, William greenlit the team to create a launch plan in three test markets. Once they saw traction in those markets, they'd be able to make the go/no-go decision about launching across the country.

After you've run tests, you too will have a strong perspective on your most effective messages. It's time to go back to your messaging framework and make revisions that ensure your messaging is launch-ready for your persona. Next, you'll learn how to create a powerful product narrative out of your messaging framework.

STANDOUT STRATEGIES:

- Get customer feedback on your updated messages through interviews and sales conversations so you can refine your messaging framework.

- Run tests to measure actual customer behavior when they see your new messages in emails, ads, and landing pages.

- Use your judgment about which new messages to roll out. Remember that you'll need to iterate, and messages rooted in your 3 Ps are more likely to win in the long run.

CHAPTER 11

DEVELOP YOUR PRODUCT NARRATIVE

All paths eventually lead customers to your product narrative.

A product narrative pulls together your key messages into a story that ends with your ideal customer knowing that your product is a good fit for their needs. It speaks to your persona and explains the problem your product solves, the outcomes it will create in their lives, and the reasons to believe it delivers results. It concludes with a compelling call to action (CTA) to take the next step.

Your product narrative forms a wireframe for your website homepage, driving your customer toward a sales call or purchase. This narrative also creates a powerful structure for your sales conversations. It resonates emotionally with your ideal customers and also backs up your claims and promises with logical proof points. Everything you've drafted up until this point will serve as ingredients for a narrative that increases customer desire and preference for your product.

Caroline, the CEO of the accounting software startup (from chapter 5) needed to build and roll out her company's product narrative. While the startup was effectively attracting new customers through paid ads and influencer marketing, Caroline was concerned about the conversion rate on her startup's homepage.

As we looked at the company's website, there were some clear gaps. The website talked about the product's features but did not share anything specific about who the product was for or why it was better than well-known solutions.

Even though customers were raving about their experience using the accounting app, the site did not include clear value props, customer success stories, or a demo of the product. While the homepage did have a call to action to start a free trial, prospective customers weren't finding the information they needed to make a decision to sign up. Caroline was quickly able to improve this with a product narrative. I'll show you how to create one in this chapter.

As you read through effective startups' websites, you'll see that many follow the same storytelling formula. The homepage leads with a hook and USP. The next section focuses on three value props, and additional modules back these up with social proof and other proof points that the product can deliver this value. You've already developed each of these elements. Now you can easily create an effective product narrative that moves your ideal customer from curious to convinced that your product is right for them.

CONSTRUCT YOUR PRODUCT NARRATIVE

A product narrative captures your ideal audience's attention, gains their trust, and helps them understand why your product is best for them. A strong product narrative makes a company's ideal customer the protagonist of the story, mainly using "you" to refer to the customer, not "we" (to refer to the company). Rather than explaining what "we" do, a strong product narrative explains how we help "you."

Strong product narratives include these components, in the following order:

- **Hook:** Capture attention and drive interest from your ideal customer so they want to learn more.

- **Problem empathy:** Demonstrate that you understand the key pains your ideal customer experiences.

- **USP:** Explain what your product does, who it's for, and how it's unique in a powerful headline.

- **Value propositions:** Share the appealing, differentiated benefits your product delivers.

- **Proof points:** Validate and support each value prop with compelling reasons to believe.

- **How it works:** Overview the unique way your product achieves results.

- **Stakes:** Recap the consequences of not acting now to create urgency.

- **Call to action:** Share the clear next step you want your ideal customer to take.

Think about each element of your product narrative as a module. You can easily update these modules as you test or update your messages. You can try different hooks, variations of your value props, and fresh proof points within your narrative. Your goal is to continue to refine the story to increase engagement and conversion anywhere you use it to attract interest: your website, sales deck, emails, pitches, and more.

Now let's dig into the role of each piece of the narrative and how to construct your modules.

HOOK

The opening of your narrative needs to grab your ideal customer's interest. You'll use a hook in the hero module of your website or as the opening of your sales presentation. Strong hooks accomplish two main things:

✦ **Captivate your ideal customer:** A hook signals to your ideal customer that this content is for them, and it captures their attention.

✦ **Open a loop:** A hook leaves a question unanswered or intrigues your ideal customer to learn more. A strong hook creates interest and curiosity that the customer can't resist indulging.

In chapter 16, you'll learn all about how to craft enticing hooks. As a starting point, know that a strong hook may:

✦ Highlight an exciting benefit or result that your product delivers.

✦ Mention an urgent challenge or pain point that your audience is facing.

✦ Preview the unique way your product addresses a pain point.

I'll reveal the accounting software startup's product narrative as we go along, starting with the hook. Caroline's ideal customer was a professional services business owner who needed to track time, invoice monthly, and maximize tax and retirement savings. As you saw in chapter 5, Caroline and her team realized that their powerful invoicing capability was particularly attractive to their ideal audience. They used this hook, leading with a desirable result.

Hook: Accounting Software
Automated smart invoicing, so you maximize revenue.

PROBLEM EMPATHY

Once you have your target customer's attention, you want to show empathy for their challenge or unmet aspiration. Confirm that you understand what's hard, confusing, frustrating, or painful for your ideal customers today. Affirm your customer's unfulfilled desire or aspiration. On your website, you may add your short positioning statement to your hero module, right after the hook. This statement explains who your product is for and implies the problem it solves. You could also create a module that speaks directly to your persona's pain points. That's what Caroline's startup did with the "problem empathy" messaging below.

In a sales deck, you'll likely go into more detail about the current challenges your ideal customers face and the consequences. This section builds connection and trust with your persona. It makes them realize your company understands where they're coming from and establishes your startup's expertise. Problem empathy also creates anticipation for what you have to offer that will solve their problem.

Problem Empathy: Accounting Software
Staying on top of invoicing is time-consuming and complex. When you let it slip, your revenue takes a (major) hit. You want to make payments a breeze for your business and your customers.

SOLUTION

At this point, your ideal customer is open to hearing about the solution you have to their challenges. Introduce your product and lead with the outcome you promise. This is a great time to state your USP, sharing the result your product delivers and its key differentiators. Go beyond explaining the functional pains your product eliminates and share the emotional gains your persona will experience, too. After this, you'll transition into explaining your product's top benefits through your value props.

Solution: Accounting Software
[Product] is an all-in-one accounting solution for professional services businesses. Smart invoicing makes sure you get paid for every hour you work. You'll get easy expense management and smart tax prep, too.

VALUE PROPOSITIONS

Now it's time to introduce your value propositions. They'll help your ideal customers quickly understand the top benefits your product offers. When combined, these value propositions create extraordinary, differentiated value for your ideal customers. You've crafted your value props to create desire and an emotional connection. Value props help your ideal customer imagine the positive impact of having these results in their life. By this point, your persona is interested in what you have to offer, but they need to see that your product is the best choice for them.

Value Propositions: Accounting Software

✦ **Get paid:** The most effective invoicing to ensure you get paid.

✦ **Profit management:** Easy expense management so you can earn more.

✦ **Tax savings:** Maximize tax savings automatically.

PROOF POINTS

Next, you'll use your range of compelling proof points to support each value prop, building trust and credibility. In your messaging framework, you've already mapped out supporting stories, data, endorsements, and FAQs to validate each value prop. These proof points will be the basis of multiple modules on your website, and you'll include them throughout your sales deck, too.

As you learned in chapter 9, weave in proof points that are the most credible and motivating for your ideal audience. You want to proactively overcome their objections. These proof points can include quotes, testimonials, case studies, data points, claims, media coverage, endorsements, and more. One more tip: Add proof points earlier in the narrative as well, so you build credibility from the start. For instance, you may want to share a compelling customer quote after your USP to show how satisfied customers are with their results.

Here are the proof points the accounting software used to validate their value propositions.

Proof Points: Accounting Software

Get paid
The most effective invoicing to ensure you get paid.

✦ **Features:** integrated time tracking, effortless invoice preparation, automatic receivables follow-up, invoice payment reports

✦ **Social proof:** "I used to chase clients for weeks or forget altogether. [Product] never misses a follow-up, so I get paid every time"—Customer, location, business name

✦ **Data:** Customers report a 55% increase in getting paid within 30 days of the invoice due date.

Profit management
Easy expense management so you can earn more.

✦ **Features:** forward receipts to your virtual expense concierge, expenses are auto-categorized, costs are easily allocated to clients

✦ **Social proof:** "For the first time, I no longer have untracked expenses in my inbox. I forward them on, and [product] makes it effortless to keep track of everything I spend by each client."—Customer, location, business name

✦ **Guide:** Check out our "Smart Expense Guide" video to see exactly how [product] manages expenses so you don't have to."

Tax savings
Maximize tax savings automatically.

✦ **Features:** tax savings maximizer toolkit, retirement savings generators, easy reporting in a click, automated tax doc prep

✦ **Social proof:** "I've automatically saved hundreds of dollars in annual taxes thanks to [product's] tax toolkit. I had no idea what I was missing."—Customer, location, business name

✦ **Endorsement:** Accounting magazine quote: "Customers say it's like having an expert accountant implementing all the right tax strategies and getting invoices paid."

HOW IT WORKS

As part of your proof points, give a clear overview of how your product works. Develop a simple framework or a few steps to explain the unique way your product delivers results for customers. This framework will help differentiate your product from the other solutions they consider. It will also help your ideal customers picture themselves using your product and getting results. Plus, they'll know what to expect when they start using your product.

How it Works: Accounting Software
Note: accompanied with demo and product visuals

✦ **Automatic invoices:** Set up clients and track your time. Then let [product] send invoices and follow-up so you get paid.

✦ **Effortless expenses:** Email expenses to your virtual concierge. Everything gets auto-categorized and allocated to the right client.

✦ **Real time reports:** Generate reports with just one click, so you always know how you're tracking against your goals.

✦ **Lower taxes:** Quarterly tax filings get prepared with expert strategies, so you capture smart tax savings.

STAKES

As you approach the end of your narrative, you can create urgency and motivate your persona to take the next steps by recapping the stakes of their decision. Share the stakes in two ways:

✦ **Opportunity cost:** Remind your ideal customer of the big benefits they'll miss out on if they don't act now. Recap the upside of moving forward with a solution and the positive changes that await.

✦ **Negative consequences:** Remind your ideal customer of what they stand to lose in their lives or business if they keep postponing action or choose a suboptimal solution. Reassure them that your product ensures they'll avoid those consequences.

Stakes: Accounting Software

✦ Never miss out on getting paid again. Increase your revenue and maximize profit.

✦ Stop spending time on accounting. Make invoicing clients, managing expenses, and tax prep a breeze.

CALL TO ACTION

End the narrative with a clear, bold call to action that directs your prospective customers to take that next step. Before you create a website, sales deck, or email series, decide exactly what you want your ideal customer to do once they reach the end of your product narrative. For instance, this could be "start now" (download the app, sign up now), "learn more" (download the guide, watch the video), or "book a call" (request a demo, meet with sales). Weave this clear CTA throughout your homepage, and make sure it's in the last module before your website footer, too.

CTA: Accounting Software
Start free trial

With that, you have a narrative that takes a prospect on a journey to understand why your product is right for them and how it will deliver the results they need. Your foundational messaging is almost complete. But there's one more element to revisit. You've likely already developed company messaging, including a vision, mission, and values to guide your startup. In the next chapter, we'll talk about how to revisit these messages to ensure they align with your 3 Ps and messaging progress.

STANDOUT STRATEGIES:

‣ Create a product narrative, turning the pieces of your messaging framework into a story that guides your ideal customer through the value of your product.

‣ Build an emotional connection with your ideal audience when you open with a strong hook, show problem empathy, and introduce your solution in a compelling way.

‣ Showcase your value props and a range of proof points that validate how your product delivers results. Create urgency when you close with attention-grabbing stakes and a clear CTA.

PRODUCT NARRATIVE TEMPLATE

HOOK

Hook the attention of your target audience with a catchy headline that creates an open loop.

PROBLEM EMPATHY

Show that you understand the pain points and needs of your target customer. Empathize and relate.

SOLUTION

Share a concise, powerful overview of who your product is for and the results it delivers (USP).

VALUE PROPOSITIONS

Share the three value propositions that showcase your product's unique benefits.

- 1
- 2
- 3

PROOF POINTS

Share customer stories, data, and endorsements that support your value propositions.

- 1
- 2
- 3
- 4
- 5

HOW IT WORKS

Share an overview of how your product works, including a step-by-step framework and key features.

- ✦ 1
- ✦ 2
- ✦ 3
- ✦ 4
- ✦ 5

STAKES

Restate the positive results your customer will achieve or the negative consequences they'll avoid.

CTA

Motivate your ideal customer to take the next step (learn more, sign up, buy, etc.).

CHAPTER 12

REFINE YOUR COMPANY MESSAGES

How does your product messaging connect to your overall company messages? Your company messaging includes your vision, mission, and values, and they detail your startup's purpose and guiding principles. Your new USP and value props speak about your product's differentiated value and the outcome it delivers for customers. Together, these messages demonstrate why your company exists and how your product creates positive change for customers. They are interrelated. Once you have new product messages you'll want to update your company messages, too.

You articulate your startup's goals and how you achieve them in three main company messages:

✦ **Vision:** "Why" does your company exist? What is the impact it seeks to create in the world?

✦ **Mission:** "What" does your company do? How does it drive results for your ideal customers?

✦ **Values:** "How" does your company operate? What ideals and guiding principles drive the team?

You likely created your company's vision, mission, and values in the early days of launching your startup and pitching investors. With renewed clarity on your 3 Ps and product messaging, you may be able to express your purpose and ways of working in words that more deeply resonate with your ideal customers and the outcomes you create. Now is a great time to revisit these messages and decide what to update.

To refine your company messaging, think boldly and over a longer horizon than you may have done to craft product messaging. These messages need to highlight not only the transformation you create for each customer but also the positive impact your company makes in broader society. Consider the mindsets and behaviors your company embodies to make this vision and mission a reality. Now let's dive into each part of your company messaging.

REFINE YOUR VISION STATEMENT

A vision statement describes "why" your company exists and clarifies your startup's long-term goal. It sums up your company's ultimate ambition in the world and describes what a better future looks like for your customers, your stakeholders, and society once your vision becomes a reality. Your vision captures your startup's driving purpose.

In most cases, your company cannot achieve this bold vision alone. It's part of a bigger movement that involves multiple companies and solutions. Your product and your customers' results play an important role in driving progress toward this new reality. In your vision statement, paint a picture of what the world will look like as you achieve your goals. Vision statements are often aspirational, inspirational, and purpose-driven. They are durable, capturing your company's ultimate goal over many years. If your view of the future has evolved, now's a great time to reflect that in your vision statement.

Strong vision statements are concise and punchy. Ways to start a vision statement include:

+ We envision a world where...
+ Our vision is to create...
+ We exist to...

For a diversity, equity, and inclusion (DEI) platform that I advised, refining their vision made sense after we updated their product messages. Their updated vision was "to create workplaces where all people can be leaders and thrive." The startup knows that today, many people do not feel a sense of belonging in their companies, and only a select few stand a chance of advancing into upper management roles. The startup's new messaging emphasized that its product is a holistic solution to DEI. They were not satisfied with just helping their customers hire a more diverse workforce; they wanted to help all types of employees get promoted to leadership levels, too.

REVAMP YOUR MISSION STATEMENT

A mission statement describes "what" your company does and how your startup makes progress toward your vision. Your mission is connected to your USP, describing who your product is for, the outcome it offers, and how it delivers results in a differentiated way. While mission statements can be bold and ambitious, they should also describe what your company and your products can actually help customers achieve.

Mission statements need to be updated more often than vision statements, especially if your product evolves quickly. "What" results your product delivers, and how you drive this change, will get more powerful as you launch the features on your product roadmap. As your product's benefits and functionality improve, your mission statement can get more ambitious.

When the DEI platform reconsidered its mission, the startup knew it offered its customers a comprehensive set of tools to hire, retain, and advance a diverse workforce. They also wanted to help leaders measure the impact of their efforts. They needed a mission that explained how their solution creates systemic, sustainable change at companies (unlike some other platforms, which only address a part of the employee journey).

The startup followed this mission statement formula:

+ We [what your product does]
+ for [ideal customers]
+ to [outcome your product delivers]
+ through [product description].

They developed this mission:

We [offer a holistic DEI platform] for [high-growth companies] to [increase retention and advancement, so anyone can achieve and thrive in leadership positions] through [automated tools, playbooks, and success tracking for the entire team].

Along with updating your vision and mission, you'll want to reconsider your company values to ensure they explain the principles that guide your team.

REVISIT YOUR COMPANY VALUES

Your company values describe "how" your company operates to achieve your vision and mission. Company values are the principles by which you accomplish your goals. Values capture how your team members work together, which drives company culture. Your values also highlight how your startup builds for and engages with your ideal customers. Your company values must align with the needs of your ideal customers.

Company values are a guiding light for your team and will shine through in your messaging and brand. They inspire the way your company and the team create a strong customer experience and deliver results.

The DEI platform embraced these company values:

+ **Empathy for all employees:** They aimed to understand the challenges and circumstances of a wide range of employees at their ICP to design an effective product experience.

+ **Real talk for real results:** They dealt with highly sensitive issues that impacted peoples' careers and lives. They recognized that some of their recommendations would be uncomfortable. This value confirmed that customers could expect "straight talk" to help them make real progress toward goals.

+ **Collaboration creates change:** The team needed to effectively collaborate to build a transformative product. They also needed to collaborate seamlessly with their customers to drive change.

To help you decide how to update your vision, mission, and values for your company, imagine a description of your company's success a couple of years into the future. You'll find an exercise to do this in the next section.

IMAGINE FUTURE PRESS COVERAGE

To think longer term about your mission, vision, and values, outline an ideal article you'd like a reporter to write about your company two years from now. Your team will have made progress toward your mission and vision, embodying your company values along the way. This article raves about your company's successes, strong growth, customer results, and broader impact. This will help you crystallize what impact your company exists to create. Answer these questions:

✦ What media outlet publishes this article?

✦ What's the headline?

✦ What big results has your company created for your customers?

✦ What broader impact has your company created in the world?

✦ What values did your company follow to accomplish these results?

✦ What does the article applaud most about your company?

✦ How would your top customers describe your product?
   • What transformation did your product create in their lives?
   • What do they like best about your product?
   • What do they like best about working with your company?

Consider these insights, along with what you've learned from your 3 Ps and product messaging, to refine your company messages. With that, you can feel confident that your vision, mission, and values convey your purpose and guiding principles. Fill in your updated statements on the *company messaging* template at the end of this chapter.

Once you're here, you've reached an exciting point. You now have a strong product messaging framework, a clear product narrative, and refined company messages. That said, you may be wondering how to efficiently tackle the work we've covered up to this point in the book. That's exactly what I'll overview in the next chapter! I'll walk you through how to accomplish everything we've discussed during six sprints that span 12 weeks. Turn to chapter 13 to get this project plan to create significantly stronger messaging for your startup in just one quarter.

STANDOUT STRATEGIES:

‣ Revisit your company messaging after you refresh your 3 Ps and product messaging. Make it clearer or bolder with your new insights.

‣ Develop a vision statement that explains your company's purpose and the broader impact your startup aims to create in the world.

‣ Create a mission statement that's aligned with your USP and explains what your company does to help your customers and achieve your vision. Then define values that describe your startup's guiding principles.

COMPANY MESSAGING TEMPLATE

VISION

"Why" does your company exist? What is the impact it seeks to create in the world?

+ We envision a world where…
+ Our vision is to create…
+ We exist to…

MISSION

"What" does your company do? How does it drive results for your ideal customers?

+ We [what your product does]
+ for [ideal customers]
+ to [outcome your product delivers]
+ through [product description].

VALUES

"How" does your company operate? What ideals and guiding principles drive the team?

+ 1
+ 2
+ 3
+ 4
+ 5

PRESS COVERAGE IN 2 YEARS

Imagine an ideal article that's published two years from now. It talks about your vision, mission, and values.

+ What's the headline?
+ What big results has your company created for your customers and in the world?
+ What values did your company follow to accomplish these results?
+ What does the article applaud most about your company?
+ How would your top customers describe your product?

CHAPTER 13

BUILD YOUR PROJECT PLAN AND TEAM

You now know the steps to develop powerful product messaging. As a startup leader, you might be thinking, *I need to move quickly. What's the best way to do this work, and what's a realistic timeline if we go for speed?* Also, you may be wondering who exactly to involve in this process, especially if you don't have a marketing team yet. In this chapter, I lay out both a project plan and a team recommendation to help you confidently move forward.

In the next section, I break down the steps I've outlined in the book so far into six sprints over 12 weeks. Creating new messaging in three months is an ambitious timeline, but you can make significant progress in one quarter. I encourage you to add an extra week or two to any step that you need more time to complete. This will depend on how much you know about your 3 Ps going into this process and your team's capacity to do the work, too.

If you already have a strong understanding of your ideal customer and competitors, you may be able to move more quickly through developing your 3 Ps. When your product, sales, and marketing team have many of the insights you need, you can consolidate the information and rapidly start creating your messages. That said, if your team has a limited understanding of your persona, competition, and brand personality, this whole process will take more time. Use this sprint plan as a starting point and adjust it to your needs.

MESSAGING SPRINTS IN A QUARTER

This project plan lays out the messaging development process in six sprints over a quarter. You can use these steps to structure your messaging work and make fast progress. It will give you clarity on the sequence of actions to take and a sense of how much time you'll need to complete each piece. You can download all of the templates in this book at **allysonletteri.com/toolkit** to kickstart your project.

The overview below details each sprint. Then I'll share how Sophia's e-commerce security platform (from chapters 2 and 3) followed this plan and developed its messaging in a quarter.

SPRINT 1 (weeks 1 & 2):
Develop your ICP, personas, and competitive map.

- ✦ Draft your ICP and personas, filling in details with your team.
- ✦ Draft a competitive map, creating a shortlist of competitors and capturing insights.
- ✦ Decide where you have gaps in understanding and what research to complete in sprint 2.
- ✦ See chapters 1, 2, 3, and 4 for guidance.

SPRINT 2 (weeks 3 & 4):
Complete customer and competitor research to fill in gaps.

- ✦ Conduct customer research to better understand your persona's five factors.
- ✦ Conduct competitive research to identify your top competitors' differentiators.

✦ Refine your persona and competitive map to prepare for sprint 3.

✦ See chapter 5 for guidance.

SPRINT 3 (weeks 5 & 6):

Develop positioning and a USP, and complete personality discovery exercises.

✦ Create a "status quo" positioning matrix using insights from your persona and competitive map.

✦ Work through the "flip the matrix" exercises, create a new positioning matrix, and craft a USP.

✦ Host a workshop to complete personality discovery exercises and summarize insights.

✦ See chapters 6 and 7 for guidance.

SPRINT 4 (weeks 7 & 8):

Finalize your brand personality, then draft value props and proof points.

✦ Select brand personality attributes and develop your tone of voice.

✦ Create a draft of your value props and refine it with the value prop checklist.

✦ Develop proof points to support and validate your value props.

✦ See chapters 7, 8, and 9 for guidance.

SPRINT 5 (weeks 9 & 10):

Develop and launch messaging tests.

✦ Conduct customer interviews and sales pitch tests, then make initial refinements to your messaging.

✦ Develop messaging tests and prepare to launch across landing pages, ads, emails, research, etc.

✦ Monitor, iterate, and optimize test collateral based on test data.

✦ See chapter 10 for guidance.

SPRINT 6 (weeks 11 & 12):

Synthesize test results, update your messaging, and create a product narrative.

✦ Finish and synthesize insights from your tests to decide which messages perform best.

✦ Incorporate insights into your messaging framework and refine your USP, value props, and proof points.

✦ Develop your product narrative and update company messaging to align.

✦ See chapters 11 and 12 for guidance.

Now you can see how the full messaging development process fits together. You'll be able to make rapid progress, especially if you start with a hypothesis about your persona and competitive landscape in the first sprint. To see this process in action, I'll walk you through how Sophia and her team developed messaging for their e-commerce security platform over three months.

In **SPRINT 1,** the team tapped Sophia's deep experience from working with their ICP, which was a mid-market e-commerce company that sold physical products. Then they crafted a persona for their primary buyer (the engineering director). They also completed a competitive map, identifying their top competitors' differentiators and getting clear on what made their security product stand out. By the end of this sprint, they had filled in templates for their ICP, the three personas on their buying committee, and a competitive map. They decided to focus on the "primary buyer" persona for the rest of their sprints, picking up insights about the other personas along the way. At the end of sprint 1, the team decided what additional research they needed to do in sprint 2.

In **SPRINT 2**, Sophia's team dove into research. They spoke with five engineering directors to better understand their attitudes toward security software, their unmet needs, and their perspective on each competitor in their space. Marketing and sales worked closely together to map out why engineering directors are drawn to one product vs. another. The team came to understand what ultimately makes engineering directors choose their startup's product. The team also spent time reading through competitors' websites, watching their webinars, and downloading content. Plus, they read through feedback and posts in online forums that engineers frequented. By the end of this sprint, the team had significantly refined their persona and competitive map.

In **SPRINT 3**, the team held both a positioning workshop and a personality workshop. To position their product, the team worked through the "flip the matrix" exercises. They found that they could position their product as the best option for e-commerce companies with lean teams who prioritized ease of use *and* comprehensive threat detection. With other platforms, e-commerce companies could not achieve both of those benefits. The team crafted a strong USP to convey its unique promise and differentiators. In their personality discovery workshop, the team became much clearer on how to best describe their brand and what attributes would build affinity with their ideal customers. Finally, the team prepared for sprint 4, when they developed their brand attributes and tone while also crafting value props.

In **SPRINT 4**, the team landed on these brand attributes: confident, calm, elegant, efficient. They wanted a brand personality that emphasized how the easy-to-use platform kept data security under control, so the engineering directors could stay confident and calm. The team also developed their tone of voice guidelines, wanting their content to sound articulate and authoritative but still approachable. By this point, the team also felt prepared to develop value props and proof points, completing a draft of their messaging framework. Their new messaging emphasized the benefits of their product, including ease of implementation and use, comprehensive threat monitoring and detection, and fast recoveries when breaches occur. They created a shortlist of proof points to gather, including customer quotes, case studies, and data on the effectiveness of their monitoring system. After this, the team was ready to test messaging in sprint 5.

In **SPRINT 5**, the team spent another week talking to engineering directors and getting feedback on their new messaging framework. They updated some of their value props and proof points. Then they had the sales team try out the new messaging during sales calls. The sales team saw positive results, with more conversations leading to a second booked call or a request for information that the engineering directors could share with their CEOs. This increase in conversion was exactly what the startup's team was looking for. They also launched an email test, going back to some of the directors who'd expressed interest in the product but had not booked or completed a demo call. They wanted to see if the new messaging could re-engage these prospects since it told a more compelling story about their product. As the team wrapped up tests, they moved into sprint 6 to finalize their messaging and get ready for roll-out.

As they started **SPRINT 6**, the team reflected on how much progress they'd made in one quarter. They incorporated what they learned from the sprint 5 tests into their messaging framework. Sophia felt confident about creating a product narrative as the basis for website and sales deck updates. The team was also ready to create a launch plan to update their messaging throughout their marketing and content (which we'll cover in more detail in part 3). Overall, Sophia and her team felt very clear on their ideal audience's needs, their product's unique positioning, and their brand personality. They were all aligned around a strong product messaging framework that better engaged and converted engineering directors. Each of these milestones was a win for the team, their customers, and the business.

As you prepare for your sprints, you'll need to decide who from your team will drive and participate in this work. Since you have many competing priorities, it's important to consider who can most effectively engage in this project. In the next section, I recommend who can lead the messaging development process depending on the structure of your team.

RESOURCE THE MESSAGING TEAM

Founders often ask, "How can we resource this? Who's the best person to lead this work?" The answer depends on who you have on your team today, their skill sets, their capacity, and how quickly you want to move. Multiple people could drive this work using the guidance in this book (All the steps and templates are here waiting for them. Remember the mindset "don't get stuck"). That said, you will increase your chances of success if you select a clear project leader who will own the process and be accountable for delivering results in each step.

I often see early stage startups' marketing teams evolve through several stages. Depending on which stage you're in, the best project leader could be you as the founder or another member of the team.

If you're still "pre-marketing." If you're a pre-seed, seed stage, or even Series A startup, you may not have a marketing team yet. In this stage, you as the founder are often the team's first product marketer. You'll guide your startup through the process of developing your product messaging and brand. This book gives you the structure and guidance to lead this process.

Remember that, since your company will refresh your 3 Ps, messaging, and content strategy multiple times, the process for developing messaging is a skill set worth learning as a founder. You'll get very attuned to your customers and competitors as you create your messaging and marketing strategy. This will also set you up to be a more effective coach and approver in future rounds of the process. The information you gather will guide the product development process, too.

I've coached numerous early stage founders on how to run this process, and one of the hardest parts for them is finding the time to go through each step. Once you have your messaging complete and want to launch it throughout your marketing, it can help to bring in key contractors with specific expertise. These include:

+ **Copywriter:** They will take your messaging framework and create customer-facing, polished copy in your brand tone of voice. A copywriter can also create the content for any of the collateral you test and then launch, like landing pages, emails, and articles.

+ **Designer:** They can help you create your visual brand identity and marketing collateral. Most marketing touchpoints require a designer, and they'll enable your team to launch consistent, branded collateral.

One other note: You can empower another non-marketer on your team to drive this work instead if that will help you move forward more quickly. Tap the leader of sales, customer support, product, operations, or another function and ask them to lead the process laid out in this book with your partnership. Sprint 1 starts with creating a hypothesis-driven persona and competitive map. Enlist your team's help to fill in these details.

If you have a small (or one-person) marketing team. You may already be at the stage where you've hired your first marketer. While a startup's first marketer is likely responsible for many elements of your marketing strategy, they tend to skew towards one of two roles: a product marketer (PMM) or a demand generation marketer (at B2B companies; this role is often called a growth marketer in B2C companies). Depending on which person you have on your team, you may approach this project differently.

Product marketers typically own the positioning and messaging process for a company. They also handle sales enablement, new-user onboarding, and feature launches. If you already have a PMM on your team, it's a natural fit to have them manage this process. As a founder, you now have a significant advantage after reading this book, because you know what to expect and can spot any gaps in the process. You can also share this book with your PMM so they can fast-track their planning and use the templates to accelerate their progress. Even if you have a PMM on your team, realize that they're stretched in many directions if they're managing your entire marketing strategy. Empower your PMM to hire a copywriter and designer too so they can move faster and have help with creating collateral.

Demand generation and growth marketers are responsible for attracting your ideal customers, qualifying leads, and acquiring new customers. These marketers need to understand your persona, positioning, and personality to develop an effective acquisition plan. But they often rely on a PMM to equip them with the 3 Ps and messaging, and they may feel less comfortable running this process because it's not typically in their core skill set. They'll need more guidance, coaching, and support (and this book!) to run the project. Enable them with the same contractors, too.

If you have a marketing leader and team. Over time, you'll hire a marketing leader to run your marketing team. The team may include a PMM, demand generation/growth marketer, content marketer, and more. You may have hired a dedicated copywriter and designer, too. Your marketing team leader will likely have your PMM run the messaging process, managing each step of the project and bringing in the right team to participate. Or the leader may decide to run the project themselves, depending on the project's scope and strategic significance to your company.

In this stage, the working team involved in your 3 Ps and messaging development process will also be bigger. There are more cross-functional team members who can contribute useful insights about your customers, competitors, and differentiators. More people need to buy into the process and your decisions. Your team can use a DACI framework (which we used frequently at Intuit) to define clear roles on the project. Make sure everyone on the working team is aware of the project, goals, and their roles.

- ✦ **D: Driver.** This is your project leader, likely your PMM. They'll manage the project from beginning to end. They involve the right people in each step, synthesize insights, and deliver results in each sprint.

- ✦ **A: Approver.** This is likely the founder or CEO who has final approval over your personas, positioning, and product messaging. Your marketing leader could be the approver instead.

✦ **C: Contributors.** This is the cross-functional team that provides information and input during the project. They contribute insights and may also help make recommendations about your decisions.

✦ **I: Informed.** This is the group of people, which may include the whole company, that you need to keep updated on progress and decisions. Bring your team along to get their buy-in and explain your decisions.

Remember that updating your persona, positioning, personality, and messaging requires change management within your company. Your updates may create significant shifts in how your team thinks about your ideal customer, market, and product roadmap, as well as how you communicate with customers. Be thoughtful about who you choose to lead the project and how you involve a cross-functional team along the way. Share the "why" behind your decisions, and ensure that teams who need to get on board and adopt the changes are included in the process.

At this point, you'll have a fully complete and tested messaging framework. This is a HUGE win because you can now make your startup stand out to your ideal customers through clear, differentiated messaging.

With this foundation, you're ready to infuse these messages throughout your marketing strategy. In part 3, I'll teach you how to turn your product messages into a content strategy that attracts, converts, and engages your ideal customers. You'll learn powerful tools that motivate customers to take action at each stage of their journey toward using your product.

STANDOUT STRATEGIES:

‣ Organize your messaging project in six sprints over 12 weeks. You can adjust the duration of sprints if you need more time to complete the work.

‣ Plan for you as the founder, or another leader, to run the process if you don't yet have a marketing team. You may also want to tap a copywriter and designer to develop collateral.

‣ Empower your product marketer to run this process if you already have one on your team. They will plan how and when to involve a cross-functional team and drive each stage of the project.

PART 3

CREATE A CONTENT STRATEGY THAT DRIVES GROWTH

CHAPTER 14

PRIORITIZE CONTENT TO FUEL THE CUSTOMER JOURNEY

Where do you need marketing to drive growth right now? Founders have replied to this question in very different ways:

"It's all about the top of the funnel and getting more leads for our sales team. Once I talk to someone at our ICP, I will close them 80 percent of the time. I just need marketing to help me book more conversations with the right people, then we'll grow!"

"We've got traffic coming in through search engine optimization (SEO), referrals, and some influencer marketing. But we're not converting people once they land on our website or the app store. Increasing sign-ups is a must for us."

"Our new users drop out quickly after subscribing, and we have to change that. We've worked so hard to get conversion up and to increase sales, but too many companies are canceling their subscription after a couple of months."

"Renewals are not as strong as we forecast. Some companies are cutting their budgets, and others just decide they don't need our platform anymore. We need to increase retention significantly to hit our revenue goals."

The good news is that effective product messaging and content can help you achieve each of the goals listed above. In this chapter, you'll learn all about the customer journey, which marketing goals align to each phase, and what content helps you achieve those goals.

A customer journey is the set of steps your ideal customer goes through to discover, consider, buy, and use your product. It's a simple but powerful framework to help you understand what your customers need, where they're facing friction, and how your marketing efforts can help. Prospective customers go from initially realizing they have a problem to solve, to finding out about solutions, evaluating their options, and deciding which solution to choose. Once your prospect converts into a customer, they go through additional phases: onboarding as a new user, then becoming an active customer, and ultimately deciding whether to renew, expand, or churn. Hopefully, your users refer other people to your product, too.

There are five phases of the customer journey; your marketing needs to accomplish different goals in each phase:

+ **Attract:** Create awareness and capture the attention of your target customers, driving **traffic** and **prospects**.

+ **Nurture:** Build trust and desire for your solution, generating **qualified leads**.

+ **Convert:** Increase confidence that your product is the right choice, driving **sales** or **sign-ups**.

✦ **Onboard:** Accelerate new users' time to value so they get results, increasing **new user retention**.

✦ **Engage:** Ensure active users continue to get value, keep using, and renew, increasing **retention**.

You now know exactly what types of customers you're trying to reach, convert, and engage. The next step is to anticipate your ideal customer's mindsets, challenges, and motivations during each phase of their buying process. You'll need to understand what hooks and nudges them forward based on where they are in their customer journey.

In this chapter, you'll learn what content drives conversion and growth in each phase so you can give customers what they need *and* achieve your business goals. Your product messaging distills the most effective way to describe the differentiated value of your product. With this as your foundation, you'll adapt these messages into engaging content that's helpful and motivating to customers at each step of their buying process.

PHASE 1: ATTRACT NEW PROSPECTS

In the **attract** phase, your ideal customer is facing challenges that your product can address. But they don't know about your product yet! Some prospective customers are painfully aware that they have a problem to solve, and they just need to find the right solution. Others don't yet realize they have a problem, but you can help them recognize their symptoms, the root causes, and how to address them. Reach your persona with content that catches their attention, helps them recognize your solution is relevant to them, and intrigues them to learn more. You'll learn more about content for this phase in chapter 18.

Your main goals in the attract phase are to:

✦ Increase these metrics: awareness, traffic, clicks, efficient customer acquisition cost.

✦ Build awareness of your product and customers' desirable results.

✦ Create interest, clicks, sign-ups, or booked calls to learn more about your product.

To attract your ideal customers and get them interested in your solution, you need to help them:

✦ Become aware of their problem or opportunity (symptoms).

✦ Understand what's causing the problem (root cause).

✦ Realize that a better outcome is possible (transformation).

You also need to understand how aware your audience is of their problem and potential solutions. The content you create will be different based on their level of awareness. Depending on the scenario, you'll want to focus your content on different topics:

✦ **Problem unaware:** Create awareness of the problem, what symptoms to look for, and the root cause. Share warning signs and missed opportunities if the customer doesn't address these issues.

✦ **Solution unaware:** Explain possible solutions and how to choose, letting prospects know the criteria to evaluate and select their best option. Highlight the ways your product meets these criteria.

✦ **Product unaware:** Introduce your product as a solution that meets their needs and highlight differentiators that make it stand out. Showcase the successful results your customers have achieved.

To attract new ideal customers to learn more about your product, you need to use a captivating hook that leads someone to enticing nurture content. Your message has to appear in a channel where your persona will see it. This could be ads, social media, press, events, search engines, podcasts, online media, referral programs, and more. Successful "attract" phase content grabs attention and leads to engaging information that makes someone stop scrolling, decide to click, or start listening.

We'll talk about how to craft an intriguing hook in chapter 16. These hooks could invite your prospect to read an article, listen to a podcast, attend a webinar, or visit your website. Here are some example hooks you could adapt to your niche:

✦ Warning signs you can't ignore—and what to do about them.

✦ Secrets to managing key symptoms—and why they work.

✦ Stories of customers overcoming frustrating challenges— and how they did it.

✦ Must-haves in an ideal product—and why they matter.

✦ Trends in how to solve a certain problem—and how your product is on the cutting edge.

As I worked on this phase with Lucas, whose recruiting platform you met in chapter 4, we knew his startup needed to attract two types of customers: freelance recruiters *and* heads of recruiting from high-growth companies. Both personas were "problem aware" but not "solution aware." Few other platforms offered access to specialized recruiters, so their ideal customers were usually not aware that products like theirs existed.

To attract freelance recruiters to the platform, the startup needed to create awareness of their product using compelling hooks. Lucas's team used a range of paid social media ads to emphasize their value props: enjoy flexibility while earning more, close more candidates at high-growth companies, and others. Lucas was a guest on a dozen podcasts that recruiters listen to, sharing success tips for getting hired as a freelance recruiter and introducing his platform. The team also experimented with SEO articles that were optimized to drive organic search traffic when recruiters searched for new jobs and other relevant keywords.

To attract their "primary buyer" to the platform, Lucas's team invited heads of recruiting to one of the startup's monthly webinars. Their most successful webinar hook was "How to recruit twice as fast with specialized recruiters." Through a mix of social media ads and direct outreach to heads of recruiting, the startup attracted new registrations for the event and received feedback that this was an intriguing, high-value topic. Sometimes the heads of recruiting visited the startup's website instead of signing up for the webinar. On the homepage, prospects saw useful content that introduced the platform, showcased customer success stories, and explained how the product works. You'll see how to weave your value props and proof points into your "nuture" content in the next section.

PHASE 2: NURTURE LEADS

Once you have your ideal customer's attention, you'll lead them into a content experience that will **nurture** them. In the nurture phase, you'll move your prospects from being lightly "product aware" to getting to know, like, and trust your product. You'll share valuable information with your prospects so they can see the results your product delivers and decide that it's right for them. This is also when you'll highlight your product's differentiators to help your prospect understand why it's better than other solutions. Your product narrative and proof points, including customer stories, data, and endorsements, are on full display in this phase. Learn more about creating a strong nurture experience in chapter 17.

Your main goals in the nurture phase are to:

+ Increase these metrics: qualified leads, pipeline, brand affinity, and conversion rate.

+ Showcase differentiators and demonstrate the results your product delivers, creating desire.

+ Educate and help prospects evaluate your product, motivating them to buy.

Your "attract" messages lead prospects to content on a website, in an app, or into a sales conversation. There, you'll share enticing content and take prospects through the powerful product narrative that you designed in chapter 11. You'll also offer other experiences to help prospects get to know and evaluate your product, like product demos, events, videos, or the option to book a call. For B2B startups, your goal in the nurture phase is to generate "qualified leads" for the sales team. In a B2C model, you'll create desire and help customers sign-up or buy your product directly without a sales touch.

During the nurture phase, prospects need to:

✦ Recognize that your product can solve their problem and believe it can deliver results.

✦ Feel an emotional connection with and affinity for your product and brand.

✦ Be prepared for and open to a sales conversation (B2B).

When freelance recruiters clicked through one of the recruiting marketplaces's ads to learn more, they saw a landing page full of quotes and videos of freelancers talking about their positive experiences with the platform. The site highlighted how these freelancers were placing candidates at leading companies, earning more, and loving the flexibility. The startup's site also offered an "earnings calculator" that helped freelancers see how much more they could earn through the platform.

On the other side of the marketplace, marketing caught the attention of the heads of recruiting and invited them to sign up for a live monthly webinar. Lucas led the webinar and walked through case studies of companies who'd successfully hired excellent candidates in a fraction of the time it took to recruit with an in-house team. He also shared a product demo, which spotlighted recruiter profiles and showed how easily a company could find the right specialist and track candidate pipelines. Whether the head of recruiting joined a webinar or entered their email to download another piece of content, the marketing team followed up with an email series. These emails shared customer success stories and benefits of using the platform, with a CTA to "book a consultation," and talk to sales.

Examples of effective nurture content include:

✦ Clear value propositions, differentiators, and proof points to show that your product delivers results.

✦ Reports, articles, podcasts, or videos that deliver on the compelling hooks you used to attract the prospect.

✦ Diagnostics, quizzes, and evaluations that help prospects see why your product is right for them.

✦ User success stories that detail how your product effectively drove the outcomes your users needed.

✦ Endorsements from press coverage, organizations, and influencers that show your product is effective.

✦ Product demos that explain how your product works so prospects can imagine successfully using it.

Once your ideal customer has a strong feeling that your product is their best choice, they'll move into the "convert" phase.

PHASE 3: CONVERT TO SIGN-UPS AND SALES

Eventually, your ideal customer will be ready to decide whether to buy or sign up for your product. It's time to **convert** your prospect into a new user. You'll need to answer any final questions about how your product works, your pricing, and your customer support. At this stage, you'll also need to make a compelling offer and create urgency so your ideal customer decides to take action *now*. In B2C startups, customers generally sign up on their own without sales assistance. In most B2B startups, the sales team will finalize the contract.

Your main goals in the convert phase are to:

✦ Increase these metrics: conversion rate, sales, sign-ups, order value, and contract size.

✦ Close sales and generate revenue (B2B).

✦ Drive conversion to sign up or purchase your product (B2C).

During the convert phase, prospects need to:

✦ Get their final product questions answered so they can make a decision.

✦ Feel confident that they can achieve the results your product promises.

✦ Feel motivated to sign up or buy your product.

At this stage, prospects often want more functional, tactical content that helps them get clear on exactly what to expect when using your product. The recruiting platform shared a set of FAQs with freelance recruiters that addressed their most common questions about how the platform works. They also offered a self-driven demo that let recruiters check out new job opportunities and candidate tracking tools in the platform.

For heads of recruiting, the startup shared many more details through a live demo on a sales call. During the demo, the team helped the recruiting leader select a shortlist of recruiters that were the perfect fit for open roles at their company. This conversation also helped create urgency for the head of recruiting to take action and hire those freelancers while they were still available.

Examples of effective conversion content include:

✦ Side-by-side comparisons of features, benefits, and reviews of your product vs. competitors.

✦ Detailed product information, pricing pages, and FAQs to aid decision-making.

✦ Resource centers with how-to-use content that your audience can preview.

✦ Product demos and product-specific testimonials from customers.

✦ Clear CTA in each piece of content to buy, sign up, or take action.

After this phase, you have a new customer!

PHASE 4: ONBOARD NEW USERS

Now it's time to **onboard** your new customers. During this critical phase, you'll help someone learn how to use your product and get set up for a successful ongoing experience with your product. You want your new user to experience results as quickly and efficiently as possible. Create content that accelerates someone's ability to get value from and feel delighted by your product so they'll want to continue using it. In the onboarding phase, you're also training new users on how to use your product so they're more likely to experience great ongoing results, too. We cover marketing to your existing customers in more depth in chapter 19.

Your main goals in the onboarding phase are to:

✦ Increase these metrics: new user retention, active users, and customer satisfaction.

✦ Speed up the time it takes for customers to onboard and see results.

✦ Create delight and affinity for your product and brand.

During the onboarding phase, customers need to:

✦ Take the right steps to start using key features and get set up.

✦ Get value and experience results quickly so they're motivated to continue using the product.

✦ Feel relief, delight, and confidence that they will get the results they expect.

Examples of effective onboarding content include:

+ In-product tips that guide new users through the highest priority onboarding steps.

+ Email series with step-by-step instructions that walk new users through key actions.

+ Onboarding support or a community that helps new users get questions answered.

+ A get-started guide that shares the most effective way to get started and get results.

The recruiting platform realized that once a freelance recruiter and a company made their first hire through the platform, both were much more likely to continue using the product. To help onboard new freelance recruiters, the startup guided them through how to set up a compelling profile via a series of emails and in-product prompts. Effective profiles attracted companies to select these recruiters. The startup also sent new recruiters an email every couple of days over two weeks, sharing tips on how they could get started, land their first job, and close their first hire. The startup proved that new recruiters who engaged with this content found jobs and landed first hires at a significantly faster rate.

Heads of recruiting who were new to the platform received a dedicated account manager (AM) who guided them to get set up and select their first recruiter. The AMs honed a specific process to help heads of recruiting post roles and prepare their hiring managers to use the platform. The AM checked in frequently with their head of recruiting customers over their first 90 days. They wanted to ensure the company was making good progress with their freelancer to source candidates, set up interviews, and close new hires. If a recruiter was not a great match, the AM helped the head of recruiting quickly replace the freelance recruiter with a new one. The AM's top objective was to ensure new customers closed a new hire in their first 90 days using the platform, increasing the likelihood of retention.

After the onboarding phase, your goal is to engage and retain your customers for the long haul. To help customers continue to see results, you can create useful "engage" content.

PHASE 5: ENGAGE CURRENT USERS

Now that your new customer has become an active user, your goal is to ensure they continue to get value and achieve the outcomes they signed up for. While an outstanding product experience and tangible outcomes are the biggest drivers of customer retention, the right content can also drive active use, retain users, and expand accounts. You'll **engage** your users through a range of marketing programs and content, which can include seasonal campaigns, feature launches, and lifecycle marketing. We'll discuss each of these types of content in depth in chapter 19.

Your main goals in the engage phase are to:

✦ Increase these metrics: lifetime value (LTV), retention, repeat use, order size, and sentiment.

✦ Drive customer usage of product features and help customers achieve strong results.

✦ Create customer advocates, fueling word of mouth and referrals.

Active users need to:

✦ Continue to get value and results from the product and decide to renew or expand their account.

✦ Learn about and use new, valuable features that you launch.

✦ Feel affinity for your product and brand so they become advocates and fuel word of mouth.

Lucas's recruiting platform created a campaign to get recruiters to update their profiles and offer more availability when the startup saw recruiting requests spike. Lucas's team rolled out useful features to help their freelance recruiters land new jobs and better manage the candidate experience. To launch these features, the team sent emails, created in-product notifications, and shared social media updates so recruiters would try out the new capabilities.

The startup also learned that recruiting requests often surged early in the new year, as companies refreshed their budgets and were eager to hire new team members. They developed a "new year, new hires" campaign that encouraged their heads of recruiting to come back to the platform to select specialized recruiters so they could hit their hiring goals.

Examples of effective engagement content include:

✦ Tips and nudges that ensure users try key features and know how to get results.

✦ Feature launches that introduce new functionality and help customers use new capabilities.

✦ Seasonal campaigns that emphasize the most important actions to take right now.

✦ Behavioral and time-based messages that encourage customers to act.

✦ A community that connects users and your team for tips and support.

Through the rest of part 3, you'll learn useful strategies to create and launch your content for each phase of the customer journey. But first, you need to decide which phases need attention so you can improve the customer experience and achieve your most pressing goals.

SET YOUR GOALS AND PRIORITIZE CONTENT

To decide where your team needs to focus, create a *customer journey dashboard* using the template at the end of this chapter. First, assess your startup's current performance in each phase of the journey. What are your key success metrics in each phase, and how well are you achieving those goals? Where are customers delighted? Where is conversion high? When are customers confused or experiencing friction that marketing could relieve? Give each phase a "red, yellow, or green" rating based on your current success metrics and customer experience.

Once you know how well you're performing in each phase, consider where to focus your team in the next three to six months.

Where do you need to allocate time and resources to create content and launch new marketing initiatives that achieve your goals? Imagine you have 100 points to divide across the five phases, with points representing the priority of improving metrics in each phase. Allocate your points, giving more to the phases that need the most improvement and better content to increase conversion rates.

This dashboard gives you a good sense of where your current marketing strategy is working and where you have room to improve. Given that you're balancing a lean team and limited resources, you have to make choices about where to focus. Recognize that the phases where you allocated the most points need to be your priority.

Next in chapter 15, you'll create a *customer journey content map* to prioritize what content to launch to achieve your goals. You'll learn the power of a "core content strategy" that helps you develop intentional, high-performing content that fuels multiple channels. In the remaining chapters, you'll learn many powerful tools to create content and channel plans that drive conversion in each phase of the customer journey, ensuring your top product messages shine through.

STANDOUT STRATEGIES:

‣ Create content to attract your ideal customers based on their level of problem and solution awareness. Prospects need to understand their pain points before they'll consider your product.

‣ Build content for the nurture and convert phases to help prospects understand your product's value, the results it delivers, and your differentiators. Your product messaging is crucial in these phases.

‣ Help new users quickly get value with onboarding content that shows them how to get started. Engage active users with content that helps them continue to get results, retain, and recommend your product.

CUSTOMER JOURNEY DASHBOARD

PHASE	GOAL	RATING	100 POINTS
Attract	• Increase these metrics: awareness, traffic, clicks, efficient customer acquisition cost. • Build awareness of your product and customers' desirable results. • Create interest, clicks, sign-ups, or booked calls to learn more about your product.	Red Yellow Green	
Nurture	• Increase these metrics: qualified leads, pipeline, brand affinity, and conversion rate. • Showcase differentiators and demonstrate the results your product delivers, creating desire. • Educate and help prospects evaluate your product, motivating them to buy.	Red Yellow Green	
Convert	• Increase these metrics: conversion rate, sales, sign-ups, order value, and contract size. • Close sales and generate revenue (B2B). • Drive conversion to sign up or purchase your product (B2C).	Red Yellow Green	

Onboard	• Increase these metrics: new user retention, active users, and customer satisfaction. • Speed up the time it takes for customers to onboard and see results. • Create delight and affinity for your product and brand.	Red Yellow Green	
Engage	• Increase these metrics: lifetime value (LTV), retention, repeat use, order size, and sentiment. • Drive customer usage of product features and help customers achieve strong results. • Create customer advocates, fueling word of mouth and referrals.	Red Yellow Green	

CHAPTER 15

CREATE YOUR CORE CONTENT PLAN

You've prioritized goals along the customer journey and are clear on what type of content motivates customers in each phase. Now it's time to create and launch the content that influences your customers as they research, buy, and use your product. In this chapter, you'll learn about an efficient process to plan your monthly content roadmap: a "core content" strategy.

Core content is the set of anchor pieces you'll create each month to achieve the results you prioritized in your *customer journey dashboard*. The three main formats of core content are written (articles, reports, or blog posts), audio (podcasts or recordings), and video (events or recordings). Once you create intentional core content pieces, you'll adapt and share this content through landing pages, ads, emails, social media posts, event topics, press pitches, or the range of channels you use to reach your ideal customers in each phase.

This strategy enables your team to create coordinated content rather than developing pieces in silos for each channel. You'll release several high-impact content pieces each month rather than fragmented, channel-by-channel content. That will save your team time and resources. Focusing your audience's attention on core content also helps your startup create a surround sound of cohesive messages that all stem from the same few pieces. This smart strategy streamlines your content creation process and helps you achieve your goals with less content.

Most startups include two types of content on their roadmap each month: evergreen and timely.

Evergreen content builds the foundation of your customer journey. As prospects discover and learn about your product, they'll encounter your enduring, highly useful pieces of content that catch their attention, share helpful information, and increase conversion. This content tends to have a long lifespan and will only get outdated if your product or your marketing significantly changes. Evergreen content includes high-performing and timeless ads, nurture content (like articles, reports, and webinars), product messaging on your website, and onboarding guides. In many cases, search engine optimized (SEO) content, which includes articles that incorporate keywords your ideal customers are searching for, fits in this category, too.

Timely content, on the other hand, is the fresh, of-the-moment content you create that incorporates a seasonal theme, trending topic, or timely announcement. Timely content still aligns with your key product and company messages, but it uses new, topical angles to capture attention. This content may get outdated or be less relevant at certain times of the year, but it provides a boost of interest and engagement when you share it with customers at the right time. Types of timely content include seasonal articles, feature launch announcements, reports on recent trends, themed events, and more.

Now you'll create a monthly roadmap of the content you need to achieve your goals along the customer journey and generate interest. To develop a core content plan, follow these steps:

✦ **STEP 1: Map out the calendar:** Create a monthly calendar that lists marketing goals, seasonal events, company news, and product updates, all of which influence the content you'll create in the months ahead.

✦ **STEP 2: Prioritize content themes:** Prioritize evergreen and timely content themes for each stage of the customer journey that convey the information and news you need to share.

✦ **STEP 3: Choose engaging topics:** Decide the specific hook, topic, and format for each piece of content. Add these to your content calendar and start creating. We'll cover these in chapter 16.

✦ **STEP 4: Adapt your core content:** Repurpose your core content pieces to fuel multiple channels so you can reach and engage your audience along the customer journey. We'll cover this in chapters 17, 18, and 19.

Now let's dive into how to develop your content calendar.

STEP 1: MAP OUT THE CALENDAR

First, you need to identify the most important events and priorities that impact the content you create each month. Think through your marketing goals (from chapter 14) and the news you need to share with prospects and customers, including important feature launches. You'll also want to know what's happening in your ideal customers' lives and the world more broadly. This helps you pull in themes that will make your content engaging and relevant. Consider these three things that impact your content plan:

✦ **Marketing goals:** List the phases of the customer journey that you prioritized and the types of content you need to create to achieve your goals in each phase.

✦ **Customer milestones:** Consider any upcoming holidays that your ideal customers will care about, what's happening in their lives or businesses each month, and trending or seasonal topics relevant to your space.

✦ **Company news:** Identify what features and functionality you'll launch and what company announcements are relevant to customers, like entering a new partnership.

Each of these aspects influences the content you'll create. Use the *core content planner* at the end of this chapter to fill in this information. Here's a closer look at how each of these aspects influences your content.

Marketing goals. In chapter 14, you created a dashboard that highlighted the phases of the customer journey that need your team's attention. Using the *customer journey content map* at the end of this chapter for inspiration, narrow down the types of content you need to address your goals. Consider what types of content you have today, where there are gaps, and where your messaging and content are outdated. Then develop a shortlist of the content that you need to create. Examples include:

✦ **Onboarding content:** product-specific content, including how-to guides and success tips

✦ **Nurture collateral for sales:** updates to decks, sales one-pagers, and case studies for the sales team

✦ **Customer success stories:** customer stories and quotes to use as social proof throughout your content

At my past companies, creating get-started guides for new users was always an essential part of our evergreen content roadmap. During my time at Intuit, we developed onboarding content and launched contextual, in-product tips that showed new QuickBooks users how to connect bank accounts, set up invoices, and use other key workflows. We also created a set of demo videos, which we shared with new users via email, to guide them through each step. We gave new users a home base, launching a landing page filled with videos and guides designed for them. Month by month we made progress, launching new pieces on our core content roadmap.

Customer milestones. It's important to weave timely content in with your evergreen content to connect with your users based on what's happening in their lives. What do your ideal customers care about in the months ahead? What holidays and other seasonal events matter to them? What business milestones are upcoming? What topics will they be paying attention to in the media? Add these to your calendar for inspiration:

✦ **Customer milestones:** customer-specific events, such as peak sales season or holiday season

✦ **Holidays and seasonal moments:** seasonal topics relevant to your ideal customer

✦ **Trends:** trending topics and events relevant to your audience that are happening each month

When I led Pro Marketing at Thumbtack, a marketplace for consumers to find local service professionals (pros), we tracked what types of services people tended to hire at different times of the year. For instance, every spring we saw a burst of interest in hiring pros for lawn care and wedding services. We methodically planned our core content around what our ideal customers, and the media, were interested in each month. Consumers were more likely to click through and consume content about the services they were hiring that season, like "The top five people you need to plan your wedding" in the springtime.

Company news. Consider the company news, product updates, or helpful information you'd like to share in the months ahead. Add rows that capture those announcements.

✦ **Product news:** What product releases and feature launches will matter to your audience? What new integrations, partnerships, or other updates do you need to share?

✦ **Company news:** What important company news will your ideal customers care about? This could include announcing a new partnership, funding round, or executive hire that builds interest and credibility.

At Handshake, back-to-school season was a critical time of year for us to share product updates, because students were ready to start their next job searches and companies were ready to begin hiring, too. Students were open to learning about new features that could help them find relevant jobs. Companies recruiting students wanted to hear about new features that helped them identify and communicate with candidates. This was also the time of year that students and recruiting teams were most interested in our tips about how to effectively use Handshake. We planned our content to drive interest and excitement for using our product during these peak seasons.

Once you have noted each of these dates and priorities on the calendar, it's time to narrow in on your content themes for each month.

STEP 2: PRIORITIZE CONTENT THEMES

The next step is to develop themes for timely content based on seasonal events, compelling trends, and product announcements that are relevant to your ideal customers. While your evergreen content includes enduring, useful pieces that fuel each stage of your customer journey, timely content can help drive a fresh burst of customer action. When you choose relevant and current topics for your content, you're more likely to capture your ideal customer's attention.

Look across the information you captured for each month in step 1. Identify themes that could make your messages more interesting to your ideal customers based on what's happening in their lives and the season. Ask yourself:

✦ What topics would be relevant and timely for my customers each month?

✦ What trending topics could I incorporate to make my content more intriguing?

✦ What seasonal theme could I mix into our content to drive interest?

Think about whether you want to reschedule any of your company or product news to better align with the customer and seasonal calendar. You can ask:

✦ When will my ideal audience be most open to and interested in hearing our news?

✦ How can we combine our news with a seasonal theme or trending topic to add interest?

✦ How can I sequence my news and messages to make them timelier?

Add these themes to your *core content planner*. By this point, you'll have many creative ideas for content that will be highly useful and engaging to your ideal customers each month. It's important to make steady progress on your evergreen content topics while also leaving space for the fresh perspective of timely content. That way, your customers will have the right information in each step of their buying journey mixed with pieces that are compelling at that time of the year. Timely content also gives you new, compelling pieces to share with prospects and customers via email, sales outreach, and invitations to re-engage them.

Now you have a strong plan for what content to create each month and what timely themes to incorporate. As a next step, you'll create the actual headlines, hooks, and topics for each piece of content. The next chapter shares essential tips to develop hooks and content angles that draw in your ideal audience. You'll finish filling out your *core content planner*, too.

STANDOUT STRATEGIES:

› Plan your monthly core content, including both evergreen and timely pieces, that help your customers at each stage of the customer journey and enable you to achieve your marketing goals.

› Define the evergreen content that will provide the essential, compelling information your customers need as they consider, buy, and start using your product. Make progress on this roadmap each month.

› Map out key dates that are important to your customers to develop relevant, seasonal themes for your timely content, generating fresh interest in your messages each month.

CORE CONTENT PLANNER

	MONTH 1	MONTH 2	MONTH 3
MARKETING GOALS: Content to prioritize in key phases of the customer journey			
Customer journey phase #1			
Customer journey phase #2			
Customer journey phase #3			
CUSTOMER MILESTONES: Seasonal themes and important dates to your customers			
Holidays and seasonal events			
Trending topics			
Customer milestones			
COMPANY NEWS: Product launches and company news			
Product launches			
Company news			
THEMES: Ideas and topics that make your content more timely and relevant			
Key messages			
Timely content themes			
CORE CONTENT TOPICS: Topics and formats of your core content each month			
Core content #1			
Core content #2			
Core content #3			

CUSTOMER JOURNEY CONTENT MAP

PHASE	CONTENT TOPIC	CONTENT TO CREATE
Attract	Build awareness and hook interest.	
Problem unaware	Create awareness of the problem: • Explain symptoms or warning signs. • Show opportunities or consequences. • Diagnose the root cause of the problem.	
Solution unaware	Explain solutions and how to choose: • Explain how to evaluate solutions. • Highlight important benefits of a solution. • Share strong customer transformations.	
Product unaware	Highlight differentiators and success: • Show value props and differentiators. • Highlight delightful user experiences. • Share strong customer transformations.	
Nurture	Prove transformation and build affinity: • Highlight product differentiators. • Offer diagnostics and quick wins. • Prove the results your product delivers.	
Convert	Share compelling product and offer details: • Make a compelling offer. • Offer detailed product and pricing info. • Share support and FAQ content.	
Onboard	Accelerate effective onboarding and results: • Share guides and tips. • Provide support or community. • Celebrate wins and results.	
Engage	Increase usage and results, drive loyalty: • Share nudges and tips. • Create compelling launches. • Offer access and perks.	

CHAPTER 16

CHOOSE ENGAGING TOPICS AND HOOKS

After going through the content planning process, you know the key themes and content types you need to create each month to achieve your goals. As step three to create content, you need to decide the hook and exact topic for each of your core content pieces. Your topics need to capture attention and entice your ideal customers to read, listen, or watch, then take action. In this chapter, you'll learn powerful shortcuts to help you come up with intriguing content topics.

I'll walk through two tools to develop subjects for your content that will pull in your ideal audience. First, you'll learn how to create hooks that make your ideal customers take notice. Without a hook that effectively creates interest, your persona may breeze right past your content and miss what you have to share. Then, I'll introduce you to content angles that give you a range of intriguing ways to frame and present your content ideas. Using these techniques, you'll more easily create attention-grabbing topics. Paired with all the work you've done to plan pieces that are useful for your persona along their customer journey, your content will be highly valuable *and* engaging.

CREATE CAPTIVATING CONTENT HOOKS

Want to know the secret to enticing your ideal customer to read your content? Start each piece with a fascinating hook that's highly relevant to them.

At every phase of the customer journey, you need strong hooks that help you:

✦ **Grab the attention of your specific audience** so they quickly realize the content is relevant, interesting, and useful for them.

✦ **Create open loops or unanswered questions** that intrigue your persona to learn more and entice them to keep reading, watching, or listening.

✦ **Promise a solution or insight** about one of their top pain points or desired gains so the content feels immediately valuable.

In her book *Fascinate*, Sally Hogshead describes seven powerful fascination triggers—lust, mystique, alarm, prestige, power, vice, and trust—that motivate people to pay attention and take action[3]. I've adapted these into a framework of seven captivating content hooks—pleasure, secrets, security, status, control, freedom, and reliability—that you can use to craft headlines that will grab your audience's attention. These seven types of hooks spark curiosity, opening the door for you to get your messages across to your audience. Each hook has a payoff, suggesting what benefit your ideal customer will gain if they continue.

3 Sally Hogshead, *Fascinate* (New York: Harper Business, 2016).

We'll go through each type of hook in more detail, with examples of how startups use each one. You'll also find a *captivating content hooks* worksheet at the end of this chapter that gives you thought starters to create headlines with each of these techniques.

Pleasure. Entice your ideal customers with the promise of feeling better after using your product. Create vivid images of what it feels like to have relief from their pains and experience the benefits of your product. You can share a clear "before and after" scenario that creates anticipation and allows the customer to practically feel those sensations in their body.

Many tech products use pleasure as a hook when they explain how their product will relieve feelings of stress, strain, and overwhelm. At QuickBooks, we created product content that helped small business owners imagine what it could feel like to offload tedious, onerous accounting tasks. In demo videos, as these entrepreneurs saw mundane accounting tasks getting completed automatically, they could almost feel their stress melting away.

Secrets. Offering irresistible secrets is another way to hook your target audience. People want insider knowledge and access to hard-to-get information so they can get the best outcomes. They also want secret formulas to avoid mistakes, achieve great results as soon as possible, and fast-track their decisions.

The DEI platform you met in chapter 12 created content around the secrets to hiring, retaining, and promoting diverse talent in an organization. They released articles and even offered a diagnostic call to talk about their "secret formula" for creating an inclusive, high-performing workforce. They used headlines that included the "Secrets to advancing DEI at your company."

Security. When your ideal audience needs to avoid a risky outcome, the promise of security can be a magnetic hook. Acknowledge the alarm or concerns your ideal customer feels and promise a resolution. When your ideal audience is not yet problem aware, you can alert them to a threat they need to anticipate and help them understand how to stay safe. If your ideal audience is aware of the threat, you can empathize with their distress and offer a path to safety.

For a data backup software startup, many of their hooks emphasized how secure their customers' data was with their product, even if the original data got erased. They created content about the "Top ways to ensure you'll never lose your data," which intrigued companies who feared the consequences of data loss.

Status. The promise of getting prestige from using your product will also hook your audience if they can gain meaningful status. Luxury goods or services that only offer access to a select few customers often use this technique to pique interest. An application process or waiting list can create a perception of status and exclusivity. You can also show buyers how they can gain esteem through association with your brand name or other users of your product.

One startup I worked with offered a professional development program that required both clients and their coaches to apply for the program. Participants gained prestige once they were chosen to become members of the coaching platform because only well-qualified candidates were accepted. The startup used its selection process as a hook, keeping participant quality high while creating strong interest in their program and increasing applications.

Control. If your target audience feels powerless over something in their life or business, the promise of control can be a strong hook. Offer someone the ability to manage and get a grip on a persistent challenge. You can entice your audience with insights about how to contain a problem before it grows even bigger, or explain how to influence a person or situation to get a better outcome.

A startup that offered marketing attribution software led with a headline about ways businesses could "control your cost of customer acquisition." This attracted companies who wanted to rein in their advertising costs but did not know how much they were paying for customers. The startup recommended ways to track spending and attribute customers to the right channels. Then they introduced their software as a tool to help track and control marketing costs.

Freedom. Sometimes your ideal audience wants to play by new rules and gain freedom or independence. Maybe something isn't working in their life, and they need a new path forward. Startups often want customers to break free from the norms in their category, and they offer a more effective solution to a critical challenge. You can create a hook that explains the flaws of the current system and show them a path to better results.

A startup that sells to medical device manufacturers showed how their product created more mobility for patients. The startup wanted to help these manufacturers see the benefit of moving away from traditional components and using their new technology instead. The appeal of learning how to give patients more freedom made medical device decision-makers want to learn more.

Reliability. You can also hook prospects with the promise of delivering predictable and consistent results. Sometimes the most compelling hook for your customers is the promise of a solution that they can depend on every time. Show that you know why customers need a solution that is trustworthy and steadfast. The promise of peace of mind and predictable results may be the best way to catch your audience's attention.

A mental health care startup offered a new model to treat patients. Their ideal customers had tried treatment programs in the past that didn't work for them, and they still struggled to find the right solution. This startup emphasized the reliable, predictable results that their patients experienced and explained the program's unique approach that drives sustainable changes for patients.

Now that you are familiar with these seven hooks, here's a challenge. Choose a topic, then create seven different headlines, trying out each of these hooks for your audience. Then look through your list and select the hook that will be most appealing to your ideal customers. You can even choose a couple of headlines to test in your content.

As inspiration, here are examples from an article that Sophia's e-commerce security software company developed:

+ **Pleasure:** How to move from panicked to peaceful with your site's security

+ **Secrets:** Four secrets to avoiding disasters that derail your shopping site

+ **Security:** Five warning signs your security software may not catch every threat

+ **Status:** See the new way that top e-commerce companies handle site security

✦ **Control:** Four essential tools to eliminate e-commerce threats

✦ **Freedom:** Find out how to free up your team from monitoring security, forever

✦ **Reliability:** Three ways to avoid security breaches every time

For more ideas, use the *captivating content hooks* worksheet at the end of this chapter to help you craft each of these types of hooks. Incorporating the right hook into your content will add intrigue and entice your persona to consume your content. In the next section, I'll share another set of content angles that you can pair with these hooks to ensure your content engages your ideal customer.

USE FRESH CONTENT ANGLES

You can create an engaging structure for your content by choosing an idea from a starter list of content angles. These angles can kickstart your content creation process when you're trying to decide how to communicate a set of ideas in a compelling way. Almost all of these angles are useful for both evergreen and timely content. You can also adapt any of these angles to your brand personality by infusing them with your tone of voice and brand attributes. Look through your *core content planner* and choose an appealing way to share the information with your audience:

Myths. Debunk commonly held beliefs or outdated perceptions with myth-buster content. Show thought leadership and share your forward-looking outlook or new perspective on commonly held beliefs.

Warning signs. Shine a light on symptoms of a problem that your ideal customers need to detect. Share warning signs that signal they need to take action and introduce your product as a way to address these issues.

Shocking statistics. Reveal an unexpected data point that surprises your ideal customer. Invite them to learn more from the data and propose a solution to achieve better outcomes.

Power moves. Share steps your audience can take to make high-impact changes in their lives right now. Point out the root causes of their challenges and what action steps to take.

Do it like a pro. Show your users how top professionals solve the same challenges that they face. Highlight how experts tackle these problems. Case studies of aspirational clients can also illustrate the right next steps.

Surprising truths. Share things that your ideal customer may not know about their symptoms, solutions, or results that make them want to learn more. Explain how they can think differently about this issue.

From "this" to "that." Show your reader the journey from an undesirable starting point to a much better end state. Explain how your product, or following certain steps, can deliver the change.

The most popular. Share an approach that most people use to eliminate their pain. This angle offers a decision-making shortcut for many people who feel comfortable following a well-accepted approach.

Trends to follow. What are the emerging trends your ideal customer needs to know? Why are some companies trying a new approach? This angle points customers toward the future.

This toolkit equips you with a set of prompts to inspire your content. For your persona to move to the next phase of their customer journey, they have to engage with the content you create and take action. The fourth step in your strategy is to choose the channels you'll use to reach your ideal customers and adapt your core content to each one. In chapter 17, we'll focus on "owned channels" and why you need to build strong nurture and convert content for your customers before you focus anywhere else.

STANDOUT STRATEGIES:

▸ Develop engaging topics for your core content that will entice your audience to read, watch, or listen to what you share.

▸ Use the seven captivating content hooks—pleasure, secrets, security, status, control, freedom, and reliability—as a framework to craft compelling headlines and topics for your content.

▸ Tap into fresh content angles to find an engaging, fresh structure for core content.

CAPTIVATING CONTENT HOOKS

HOOK	WHAT IT PROMISES	HOOK THOUGHT STARTERS
Pleasure	Experience positive feelings and sensory pleasure	Want to feel …? Try this! Why you can't resist this feeling … Stop feeling … and start feeling …
Secrets	Get access to insider information and tips	Find out what happens after … The secrets to solving … What insiders know about … Myths and what's really true about …
Security	Avoid threats and negative outcomes	Warning signs you can't avoid … You may be missing these killer signs … Act now to avoid …
Status	Gain prestige and respect	The most prestigious option for … How to choose the most luxurious … Why celebrities can't resist … Want …? Join the waitlist.
Control	Take command over something negative	The best way to influence … The most effective way to manage … Here's how to take control of …
Freedom	Break free from rules that hold you back	These rules need to be broken … What you're missing with the old way … How to break free and do it your way … Experience the freedom of …
Reliability	Achieve certainty and consistency	Five reasons you can rely on … The most dependable solutions for … Need a no-fail solution? Try this!

CHAPTER 17

OPTIMIZE YOUR OWNED CHANNEL EXPERIENCE

Where is the best place to start updating your marketing strategy with new messaging and content? Before you take steps to attract new customers, it's critical to create an intentional, high-converting nurture and convert experience. In this chapter, you'll learn how to use your core content in the right channels to drive conversion, setting up your startup to successfully acquire new customers.

Channels are the platforms and methods you use to reach your ideal audience at each phase of the customer journey. Content is the fuel for these channels. It's what you share through your channels that influences your ideal customers' decisions and actions. Effective content shared through the right channels will attract new leads, nurture your prospects, and help you convert sales.

The channels you use to reach your ideal customers fall into four main categories:

✦ **Owned:** channels that your company controls completely (e.g., website, emails, webinars, and blog)

✦ **Earned:** channels that voluntarily mention or share your content (e.g., PR, SEO, and podcasts)

✦ **Social:** social media channels you use to engage your audience (e.g., LinkedIn, Instagram, and Facebook)

✦ **Paid:** channels where you pay for placement (e.g., digital ads, events, affiliates, and partnerships)

As you roll out new messaging and content, it's smart to optimize your channels in the order listed above. All "attract" channels ultimately lead to your owned channels, so you'll want to make sure your owned channels contain compelling nurture and convert content first. Your website, landing pages, email sequences, webinars, and other owned touchpoints need to create an easy, frictionless shop-and-buy experience for your users. In B2C products, where the sign-up process is often "self-service," content on your owned channels does the heavy lifting of convincing a customer to sign up or buy. For B2B products, content on your owned channels helps you educate and qualify leads so they're open to and prepared for a sales conversation.

With a high-converting owned channel strategy in place, you can feel confident ramping up your acquisition efforts. When you drive new prospects into your "marketing universe," you know they'll have a good experience and are set up to speak with sales or convert on their own. Once your owned channels contain valuable content, you can layer on earned and social media channels to attract prospects and drive engagement with this content. You can also ramp up SEO efforts to increase organic traffic. These channels help you get in front of relevant audiences (often at no cost) and "earn" their attention.

Finally, you can add paid channels to accelerate access to your ideal audience. With any paid channels, you have to maintain an efficient customer acquisition cost and payback period. Otherwise, it becomes too expensive to attract customers with these methods.

When you optimize your owned channels before turning on paid channels, you ensure that you'll pay less to acquire new customers. The customer journey is designed to convert. If you turn on paid channels before you have a strong nurture and convert experience, you'll likely create a "leaky bucket" of prospects that click through to learn more, then don't proceed to become qualified leads. This gets expensive.

To get the most out of your content strategy, follow these three principles:

✦ Develop a core content plan (rather than fragmented channel-by-channel content).

✦ Publish core content on your owned channels, then adapt it to and promote it through other channels.

✦ Layer on your channels in a specific order: owned, earned, social, paid.

In this chapter, we'll go deeper into how to design your owned channel experience. Your product messaging and core content take center stage in these channels. Coming up in chapter 18, I'll show you how to fuel your acquisition strategy with core content that you adapt to a range of channels. But first, let's get your owned channels set up to convert sales.

OPTIMIZE OWNED CHANNELS

As you capture the attention of your ideal customers, you'll route everyone to your owned channels. Owned channels play a huge role in nurturing and converting your ideal customers. You need to make sure there's a clear "happy path" for prospective customers to learn more about your product, understand the results it delivers, and take the next step toward buying your product. Your website, emails, and sales decks need to incorporate your new product messaging to maximize conversion. You will also publish your core content on your owned channels, where prospects can read, listen to, and view the content you design for each stage of their customer journey. You'll drive traffic to your owned channels through a range of earned, social, and paid channels.

I worked with Caroline, the founder of the accounting software (whom you met in chapter 5, and whose product narrative you read in chapter 11) to overhaul her startup's owned marketing touchpoints. The startup's website and app store page needed to be revamped with their new product narrative, including updated value propositions and new proof points. Caroline also wanted to showcase more customer stories and highlight data on the increase in revenue that customers collected through smart invoicing.

Caroline's other top priority was to create new core content that nurtured the small business owners who came to her site. She planned to offer live webinars that taught these business owners smart accounting strategies, then she'd demo the accounting product. Caroline also created blog articles several times a month with accounting tips, which she shared via email with prospective and current customers. The product team created an enhanced demo that they launched on their website.

Caroline scheduled the creation of each of these core content pieces in her content calendar and planned to launch everything over two quarters. I'll show you the steps you can take to incorporate your new product messaging and useful core content into your owned channels, too.

UPDATE YOUR OWNED CHANNELS

Since owned channels are the marketing touchpoints that you completely control, you decide the content, design, and launch timing. Now that you have new product messaging, you'll want to update your website, app store pages, email series, blogs, landing pages, webinars, event topics, video series, direct mail, and in-product content. There are many ways to refresh your owned channels to strengthen your nurture and convert experience.

Refresh your website. Update your homepage with your product narrative (refer back to chapter 11). Your website is the central hub for anyone who wants to learn more about your product, access your content, or contact sales. Make it easy for your ideal customers to see what next steps to take with clear CTAs throughout your site. You can also incorporate new keywords that you've discovered through your research to show up more often in relevant searches. Other pages you may want to update on your site include "how it works," "pricing," "request a demo," "press," "customer stories," and a blog or landing pages.

Edit your app store pages. If you have an app, you also want your listings to incorporate your refreshed value props and proof points. Update headlines, content, and visuals to reflect stronger ways to talk about your product. Incorporate powerful keywords that your prospects are searching for.

Update your sales collateral. Your sales deck and pitches are also due for an upgrade with your new product narrative. Make sure you create versions of sales collateral, such as one-pagers and case studies, tailored to each of your personas now that you understand the key messages that cut through. Build out and showcase specific proof points that create trust with each persona, too.

Launch "happy path" nurture content. In your first few months of creating core content, focus on developing the most important assets that help customers evaluate and choose your product. What are the pieces of content from your *customer content journey map* (see chapter 15) that you need to create? Focus on pieces that help customers understand their pain points, teach them how to evaluate solutions, and showcase your product's value props and differentiators. Launch a range of social proof that demonstrates real results through customer stories, case studies, and endorsements.

This is the content that you want prospects to engage with because it creates a "happy path" to discover and choose your product. Create the landing pages, posts, email sequences, and downloadable assets that are most essential to qualifying a lead or driving a conversion. You can publish in one or more content formats, including articles, videos, or podcasts, to make your assets more engaging and accessible. Having this content in place ensures all your "attract" efforts convert as well as possible.

Offer timely content to keep prospects engaged. Now it's time to add more timely pieces to your core content plan so you have fresh ways to engage with prospects each month. As discussed in chapter 15, you'll create content with relevant seasonal angles that conveys your most important messages. In the next section, I'll give you a range of ideas for how to adapt your core content to fuel more owned channels, making it easier for your ideal customer to make a decision and choose your product.

ADAPT CORE CONTENT TO FUEL MULTIPLE OWNED CHANNELS

A core content strategy enables you to fuel many channels when you create a small set of intentional content. Here are a few smart ways to repurpose core content in your owned channels to help nurture and convert your ideal customers.

Core content x3. Don't just publish your content in one format. Turn a podcast into an article and a video, too. Make a video about a report, then record a podcast. Offering the same content in multiple formats makes it possible to use the content in a range of channels and engage more people. You can also increase the likelihood of driving more traffic from SEO when you publish in a search engine—friendly format, like a blog post or landing page.

Landing page. You can create dedicated landing pages to make it easier for users to engage with important pieces of core content. Capture attention with a strong headline hook (see chapter 16) and summarize the main points of your content on this landing page. Make it easy to access or download the report, guide, video, or podcast from the page. If you require someone to give their email address to view the content, follow up with an email series that summarizes key points and introduces your product.

Email series. Share highlights and a link to your core content in an email or engaging multi-part email series. While not everyone will read or watch your longer format content, they might consume bite-sized summaries laid out in an email.

Event. Turn your core content topic into the focus of a virtual or in-person event. Share the main points of your core content via an engaging event format. You can host a panel of speakers, offer additional insights not found in the report, introduce the author of the content, and more to make the event unique and valuable.

Sales outreach. Releasing new core content gives your sales team fresh reasons to reach out to prospects and share something valuable to spark interest. The content can be a conversation starter. When you adapt the content to events or other experiences, your sales team can invite prospects, too.

Lead magnet. Consider adapting the content into a helpful resource that requires prospects to enter an email address to access it. An effective lead magnet topic helps prospective customers solve a specific, pressing problem. It also plants the seed that your product can solve their full set of pain points. Lead magnets could include a guide on how to address a challenge step-by-step, a diagnostic quiz, or access to an exclusive training.

Once you've rolled out your new messaging and core content across your owned channels, you're better set up to effectively acquire new customers. As your ideal audience lands on your website or other content, your touchpoints are ready to nurture and convert. Now you can confidently focus on amping up the "attract" phase of the customer journey, filling the top of your funnel with new leads.

STANDOUT STRATEGIES:

‣ Optimize owned channels with your new product narrative and essential nurture content. Launch new evergreen and timely content monthly to make progress toward your goals.

‣ Create an intentional content journey for prospective customers once they land in your "marketing universe" so your content nurtures and converts them or creates qualified leads for sales.

‣ Adapt core content to a range of owned channels that create more opportunities to nurture and convert customers.

CHAPTER 18

FUEL ACQUISITION WITH CORE CONTENT

Now that you've optimized your owned channels, you have two big advantages. First, you can confidently put energy and budget into attracting your ideal customers. Your owned channels are now ready to nurture and convert prospects. Second, you've created core content that you can use to fuel a range of other acquisition channels that will help you acquire new customers. You've invested in building out a "middle of the funnel" and "bottom of the funnel" experience that makes it possible to convert leads that you bring into the "top of the funnel."

How can you turn core content into pieces that fuel acquisition channels and attract new leads? You can use hooks from your core content to intrigue your ideal customer to learn more from your content and build interest in your product. In this chapter, you'll see how you can repurpose core content across earned, social, and paid channels to create a surround sound of messages and do more with less, as we discussed in chapter 15. For instance, you can turn one piece of core content into paid ads, SEO content, conference speaking topics, a press pitch, contributed content, social media posts, and more.

As Caroline, the accounting software platform CEO, developed her core content strategy, she kept "attract" opportunities in mind. When she mapped out topics for blog articles, she also developed five different social media posts for each article that would catch the attention of her ideal audience. Her team also launched social media ads inviting small business owners to Caroline's live webinars, where she shared fresh accounting tips and a glimpse into their product. The startup also recorded these webinars and created a five-part video series, which the team used as another hook in social media posts and ads to attract new leads.

Caroline's team incorporated highly-searched keywords into their blog articles and other content, so several posts rose in the ranks through organic search listings. In this way, SEO also became a traffic driver as prospects clicked on the startup's articles and landed on their website.

As Caroline's team developed a year-end campaign to attract new customers, they created a downloadable guide: "Five secrets to getting paid before you ring in the new year." The team turned this guide into social media posts and a special live webinar that Caroline hosted shortly before Thanksgiving. Plus, Caroline worked with a PR agency to pitch these "secrets" to several online business magazines. The tips got published! The startup added the article to its website as a credibility-builder and promoted the article on social media, too. This visibility led more prospective customers to download the guide and sign up for the live webinar.

You can employ these same techniques to attract the right leads to your product, too.

REACH YOUR AUDIENCE THROUGH EARNED AND SOCIAL CHANNELS

Once your owned channels are set up with useful content, you can layer on earned and social media channels to build visibility and attract new leads. Earned channels are platforms that voluntarily mention or share your content. These channels are unpaid, and you "earn" the attention of your ideal customers when your content appears there. Earned channels include press coverage, organic search, contributed content, blogs, speaking at events, and guesting on podcasts. They give your startup access to an audience that you may not be able to reach elsewhere.

Earned channels also help build your product's credibility. You won't need to explain why your product is so valuable; instead, customers see and hear trusted third parties promoting and endorsing your product. You don't have control over how or when your content shows up in earned channels. But the right content plan will maximize the chances that your top product messages will pull through, attracting new customers with these placements.

With social media channels, you have control over the content you create, what you publish, and when you publish it. You also decide how you interact with your audience and engage with others' content. But you often don't have control over who sees your content or when they see it, because the platforms call the shots. While you own the content you post, you "earn" audience engagement via social media through factors you can't fully control. Many variables influence whether you'll be able to build visibility and drive clicks from social media platforms.

How can you effectively develop content for all of these channels? I often see startups fall into the trap of creating fragmented content, building separate pieces to share through owned, earned, and social media channels. Instead, adapt the core content from your owned channels to create the assets you need for acquisition channels. This saves time and resources while also ensuring you share integrated, cohesive messages across these platforms. Resist the tendency to create pitches and posts from scratch or in a vacuum. Develop collateral using the messages and angles in your core content instead. Also, recognize that you can use any media coverage or endorsements you land as helpful proof points. Post these on your owned channels and social media, too.

One more callout on acquisition strategy: Another important lever to harness is product-led growth (PLG). The first spark of PLG is a product that delivers exceptional outcomes and delight, creating users who are excited to recommend your product to others. Virality can drive powerful growth. Plus if your product has network effects, where customers get more value from your platform when others use it too, the PLG flywheel will pick up speed. Product and marketing teams can accelerate users' referrals through paid referral programs and incentives.

You can also help your product spread the word about itself, as Caroline's accounting software did through a label that said "Powered by [product name]" stamped on every invoice her customers sent. Ideally, your product *and* customers help you acquire new users at low or no cost. Leads who find out about your product through PLG will often encounter the content you share through earned and social channels, which can boost their interest in your product. Your startup's strong owned channel experience, which you prioritized in chapter 17, will nurture and convert these interested prospects. Given this, an effective content strategy can increase conversion from product-led growth loops, too.

Now let's see how to use your core content to fuel earned and social channels.

ADAPT CORE CONTENT TO EARNED AND SOCIAL CHANNELS

There are several things to keep in mind as you develop core content that you can use to attract (and nurture) your ideal customers in earned and social channels. Let's look at ways you can adapt your core content.

PR pitches. Your timely content is often the springboard for creating relevant, exciting media pitches. You can pull out key pieces of data or craft a story angle that is timely and relevant. You want to get media coverage that positions your company as a go-to expert on topics related to your top product and company messages. You also want coverage that you can repurpose as useful proof points throughout your content.

Contributed content and podcasts. Contributed content includes anything that your team creates and shares with other media sites to publish. These channels allow you to reach a new, relevant audience. Develop a list of blogs, podcasts, or influencers that talk directly to your ideal customers. Regularly pitch new content ideas that are inspired by your core content. Offer to guest on a podcast or write an article on a topic that's an excellent fit for that platform.

SEO. You can drive organic traffic to your owned channels through content that ranks for keywords that your ideal customers search. Sometimes, you need a dedicated content strategy to generate substantial new leads via SEO. That said, every piece of content you post can follow SEO best practices to maximize its chances of ranking. Whether it's a blog article, podcast summary, or onboarding guide, your content needs to incorporate keywords and follow a structure that makes it possible to rank on the first page of search engine results and drive clicks.

Social media posts. You can generate many of your social posts from your core content and any other earned content that gets published. Turn your core content ideas into engaging social media posts through:

- **Snippets:** Share a passage, video clip, or sound bite.

- **Quotes:** Post key quotes and memorable points.

- **Summary:** Create a carousel or video of the main points.

- **Graphic:** Convey the information through a simple, visually engaging graphic.

- **Quiz:** Ask quiz questions and share results that highlight important points.

- **Poll:** Ask questions and opinions, then share the facts.

Earned and social channels both help you reach and gain credibility with your ideal customers. They can be a high-leverage, low-cost way to achieve your goals. That said, you often have limited control over how many people you'll reach and if they'll take action. Many startups also layer on paid channels to multiply the chances of attracting or re-engaging their ideal customers.

ACCELERATE REACH WITH PAID CHANNELS

You can use paid channels to get additional access to your ideal audience. While paid channels expand your reach and enable retargeting, you should layer them on as the last part of your channel strategy. Strong content in your owned channels will increase conversion rates and reduce payback periods. Investing in earned channels gives your startup strong credibility when your prospect sees positive press coverage, hears from you on podcasts, and follows influencers who endorse your product. Don't jump into launching paid channels to attract awareness and traffic until you've got the other pieces in place first.

Paid channels include any opportunities where you pay for placement to attract and engage your target audience. You often have control over the content, design, and go-live timing in these channels. With the right targeting, you can strongly influence who you reach. But you also have to pay a platform or partner for the opportunity to reach people, so this can add significant cost to your marketing strategy. Paid channels include paid search engine marketing (SEM), social ads, affiliate marketing, paid influencers, paid partner marketing, trade shows, and out-of-home advertising, plus paid placements in media, newsletters, and events.

As you design your paid channel strategy, consider these ways to adapt core content:

Social ads. Repurpose ideas from your core content into engaging social ads. You can often adapt your organic social posts to become paid ads, so revisit the earlier section on "social media posts" to get ideas for these ads. Plan and test where to drive ad traffic to achieve the highest conversion. This could include routing people to your website, a landing page dedicated to nurture content, a page to "book a demo," or somewhere else to engage this prospect.

Influencer marketing. Beyond your earned influencer strategy, you can also pay influencers and certain media outlets to feature your content. Core content gives you great ideas for things influencers can say and promote to drive interest in your product. For instance, if you release an exciting new data report, you could work with an influencer to share key details in their own unique way with their audience.

Trade shows and conferences. You can showcase the topics from your core content at trade shows, conferences, and in-person events in a range of ways. When you meet prospects at industry events, you directly share relevant core content pieces via handouts or email. You can also adapt your core content into topics for speaking opportunities and talking points for panel discussions. A core content topic could also be the focus of a small group session that you host. Having a fresh set of ideas from your core content makes it easier to share new, interesting topics at events.

Your core content holds the keys to an incredible range of assets that can fuel the channels you use to acquire new customers. Repurpose this content to reach, engage, and convert your ideal audience. Use the *content repurposing checklist* at the end of this chapter to help you consider the many ways you can adapt your content to a range of channels.

The steps I've outlined in this chapter and chapter 17 help you develop an integrated marketing plan to acquire customers. The content you create will enable you to launch and test new channels. And the channels you use to reach your audience will shape the core content you create. This content development and channel selection process ensures your ideal audience sees your key product messages and motivates them to choose your product.

Next, it's time to think about the last two stages of the customer journey: "onboard" and "engage." The marketing efforts in these phases are often called "customer marketing," which holds the keys to significant improvements in customer retention and expansion. You'll learn how to use core content to develop a strong customer marketing plan in chapter 19.

STANDOUT STRATEGIES:

› Develop an acquisition strategy that lets you attract new customers into your nurture and convert experience.

› Adapt your core content to reach your ideal audience with earned and social channels. Media coverage and endorsements can help you generate helpful proof points and earn credibility.

› Use paid channels to accelerate your reach, crafting hooks from nurture content to attract customers in these channels.

CONTENT REPURPOSING CHECKLIST

CHANNEL	HOW TO USE CORE CONTENT
OWNED	
Written/audio/video	Create core content in not just one but three content formats.
Landing page	Launch a dedicated page that makes it easy to engage with your content.
Email series	Develop an email sequence that shares the main ideas from your content.
Event	Turn core content into an engaging event topic and format.
Sales outreach	Prep the sales team to share core content and spark new conversations.
Lead magnet	Create an irresistible guide or tool that helps you build an email list.
EARNED	
PR pitch	Pitch the media with relevant and timely story ideas from your core content.
Contributed content & podcasts	Create pitches for podcasts, blogs, or other sites to share your ideas.
SEO	Follow SEO best practices to maximize the chances that your content will rank.
Social media posts	Create posts with quotes, ideas, and data from your core content.
PAID	
Social ads	Develop posts from engaging content for paid social ads.
Influencer marketing	Create fresh ways for influencers to talk about and promote your product.
Trade shows & conferences	Adapt your core content to speaking and event topics and share content pieces.

CHAPTER 19

DRIVE RETENTION WITH CUSTOMER MARKETING

How can your product messaging help with customer success and retention? Through customer marketing, where you encourage your customers to actively engage with your product to maximize the results they achieve.

Customer marketing is one of the most effective ways to increase customer retention and satisfaction. Consistent product messaging plays a key role, directing users to your product's most important features. Marketing campaigns and launches can add fresh energy to your product messages and spur customer activity. You'll remind customers of the benefits they can achieve with your product, then give them guidance on exactly how to make this happen.

Once you have a new customer, your goal is to deliver on your USP's big promise, helping users get the results they signed up for. A range of business-boosting outcomes—more product usage, increased satisfaction, higher loyalty, and accelerated referrals—are the payoff from customers getting the results they expect. Customer marketing utilizes content to ensure your customers get clear direction so they can get the most out of your product.

You can use these four types of customer marketing to engage customers:

+ **Onboarding content:** Give new users guidance on how to get started and get results from your product.

+ **Lifecycle marketing:** Share time-based or behavior-based reminders to guide customers' actions.

+ **Feature launches:** Reveal new functionality and prompt customers to use the features you release.

+ **Seasonal campaigns:** Create fresh, seasonal content to spark interest and drive engagement.

We'll get into examples of how you can use each of these techniques. First, you'll need to work with your product team to define which actions you need customers to take at each stage of their lifecycle.

DEFINE VALUABLE ACTIONS

To create effective customer marketing, you need to identify "valuable actions" that you want your customers to complete at key points in their lifecycle using the product. These are the actions that unlock the benefits and outcomes you've emphasized in your messaging. First, define a few critical stages in your customer's journey after buying your product, starting with onboarding. Then, outline other stages and milestones when customers need to use essential parts of the product.

Once you define these lifecycle stages, list the features or workflows a customer needs to use in each stage to maximize their benefits. Then write a short explanation of why each action is important. Using this lifecycle map, you can develop content to encourage customers to use the right features at the right time. You can give customers guidance on what to do when, and share why those actions are valuable.

CUSTOMER MARKETING THAT DRIVES GROWTH

There are a range of content levers you can use to drive customer engagement and success with your product. Here are some of the most useful types to create for your customers.

New user onboarding. Give clear guidance to new users so they can accelerate their time to get value from your product. You want to help new users experience results quickly, so they feel the gains they've hoped for. You also want to ensure that new users take essential steps when using your product. They need to get set up properly and feel confident to continue using it. Effective onboarding not only increases new user retention; it also often increases long-term retention, because customers learn the best way to get results from your product.

William's catering marketplace team, which you met in chapter 10, created a set of onboarding videos and sent a set of emails to caterers who'd newly joined the platform. They shared tips on how to set up a winning profile and previewed what caterers could expect when they received customer inquiries. Caterers who engaged with this content saw a significant increase in their ability to book their first job and receive their first five positive reviews. This increased retention.

Similarly, the startup sent new consumers, who signed up to find a caterer, a three-part email sequence after they downloaded

237

the app and logged in. These emails gave tips on how to find the right caterer for their needs, overviewed the range of food types available, and explained more about how to customize and tailor their order. Consumers who engaged with this content were much more likely to book a caterer and leave them a positive review.

Examples of the content that will improve new user onboarding include:

✦ Get-started guides or a resource center for new users.

✦ Email series with tips sent during a new user's first couple of weeks.

✦ Video series demonstrating how to use key product features.

✦ In-product messages and contextual tips.

✦ Push notifications with reminders and nudges.

✦ Success tips from customers sharing how to get the most from your product.

✦ Live onboarding calls with a success specialist.

Lifecycle marketing. With your customer lifecycle phases mapped out (see earlier in this chapter), you can create content that encourages customers to take valuable actions at the right times. Lifecycle marketing can include time-based reminders (e.g., after two weeks, you remind a user to take an action). It can also include behavioral-based prompts (e.g., when someone uses a feature, you prompt them to do the next step). You'll use well-timed lifecycle marketing messages to encourage customers to renew or expand their accounts, too.

For caterers, William's app sent timely reminders about completing their profile, updating menus, and responding to unopened customer messages. For consumers, the app sent push notifications around major holidays and seasonal events when families and businesses often needed caterers. Consumers could update their settings so they were only reminded about events that they cared about. After several weeks of not using the app, consumers and caterers received emails that inspired them to return to the app, offering new get-hired tips for caterers and food recommendations for customers.

You can engage customers to take action through lifecycle marketing with:

+ Time-based tips on how to use a key feature or take action in your product.

+ Triggered emails that are sent automatically after a user takes a specific action.

+ Proactive outreach from an account manager once a user reaches key milestones.

+ In-product messages and contextual tips.

+ Push notifications with reminders and nudges.

+ Customer stories showing when and why they use a feature.

+ Videos that demonstrate what to do next.

✦ Resource centers with content and tips organized by life stage or customer goal.

✦ Reminder emails to renew, expand, or add relevant services.

Feature launches. When you launch new features, you want customers to know why they're useful and get excited to use them. You'll explain how new functionality helps customers get even better results from your product. Occasionally, your new features will generate novel, differentiating benefits and you'll refresh your value props to incorporate these meaningful updates (see chapter 8 for a refresh).

When the catering app launched new features, William's team turned to their product messaging frameworks to decide how to talk about the new functionality. One of their top value props for caterers was "book customers for off-peak days." When the app released new meal-planning features for families, the startup told caterers about how this feature aimed to increase weekly family meal catering orders. Via email, in-product notifications, and social media content, the marketplace encouraged caterers to upload new weekday family menu options to their profiles to be ready for customers' increasing interest in this service.

Make your feature launches enticing for customers and encourage them to use new functionality with:

✦ Creative campaigns that draw attention to your new feature and its benefits.

✦ Social media posts that showcase your new features and results.

✦ Email series that introduce new features, their value, and how to use them.

✦ Online events where you demo and build excitement for features.

✦ Video series that demo the features and highlight the benefits.

✦ User stories that show why users like the feature.

✦ Press coverage or contributed content that highlights new features.

Seasonal campaigns. Seasonal campaigns include timely content that encourages customers to take valuable actions at relevant times of the year. With these campaigns, you'll create a fresh theme or way of sharing product messages with your customers. Seasonal campaigns can help reduce any fatigue customers feel from hearing the same messages repeated frequently in your marketing and product. These activities help you direct customers' attention to what actions matter most with a timely hook.

Since food was involved, there were plenty of seasonal moments that gave William's catering platform fresh reasons to remind customers and caterers about their service. The team launched at least one campaign per quarter, encouraging consumers to order catering for seasonal occasions. These included Thanksgiving in November, Valentine's Day in February, and graduation events in May. The startup also used these holidays to remind caterers about the valuable actions they could take to prepare for the season, including updating their profiles, adding delicious seasonal menus, and increasing their capacity to take on new orders.

Make your seasonal campaigns engaging with:

✦ Themed content that draws attention to your messages.

✦ Social media posts that promote your campaign messages.

✦ Reports or articles that communicate the value of actions in that season.

✦ Email series promoting the campaign and driving action.

✦ Giveaways and access to special opportunities.

✦ Online events that highlight the campaign theme and messages.

Creating core content for customer marketing will increase retention and customer satisfaction. You now know how to turn your messages into compelling content and channel strategies. This type of marketing motivates your customer to choose and use your products. As we move into the next (final) chapter, I'll share more about what you've accomplished and where to go from here.

STANDOUT STRATEGIES:

‣ Develop customer marketing to drive user engagement through useful content and timely reminders about what actions customers should take within your product.

‣ Create onboarding content to increase new user retention and drive up long-term retention, helping customers learn how to effectively use your product and see results.

‣ Nudge customers to use key features and improve the results they get from your product with compelling content. Launch lifecycle marketing, feature launches, and seasonal campaigns.

CHAPTER 20

CELEBRATE YOUR GROWTH

You now have the tools to create a powerful marketing strategy that unlocks sustainable user and revenue growth. You're able to run this process from beginning to end. This gives your startup an edge because you understand how to define your 3 Ps, create enticing messaging, and iterate any time your market changes.

Your ideal customer is at the heart of your messaging and content decisions, and their needs are a game-changer for your strategy. You can now explain the differentiated value of your product in a way that builds affinity and drives high-quality sign-ups and sales.

As Sophia, the CEO of the e-commerce security startup, and I wrapped up this process, we reflected on the positive changes in her business. Here are the outcomes she shared:

Aligned team. Sophia now had the tools she needed to align her team on the startup's 3 Ps and their most effective messaging for each persona. That meant that every team member had easy access to the company's best messages to adapt and use in their own initiatives. The team also participated in quarterly planning together, which meant that everyone was aligned on what parts of the customer journey to prioritize each quarter (see chapter 14).

This enabled the team to create a content plan and coordinate resources to achieve their top marketing and sales goals.

Differentiated value. A big breakthrough from this process was figuring out how to describe the value of the startup's product in a way that stood out to their ideal customers. The 3 Ps gave the team clarity on their ideal customer and their competitive landscape. They became clear and confident about how to position their product and describe its compelling differentiators. These insights translated into a unique and appealing USP, value propositions, and proof points that the team used consistently throughout their messaging.

Useful content. One of the most helpful outcomes of this process was having a framework to decide what content to create based on the startup's goals. If the team wanted to attract new customers, they knew they needed to work on hooks that led prospects to useful nurture content. If their sales conversion needed a boost, the team knew they needed to equip the sales team with useful customer stories, data, and product demos. The team updated their website, FAQs, and user stories to showcase the product's easy-to-use customer experience. Knowing what content drives conversion in each phase of the customer journey focused the team and fast-tracked planning.

Cohesive content. With a core content strategy, the team moved from creating fragmented content for each of their channels to creating a small set of intentional content that drives sales and active use. This way of developing content increased team collaboration, reduced time and resources spent, and ensured their persona saw consistent messages across channels. The team defined the startup's brand personality and infused it into their messaging and content. The startup's newly defined personality not only helped the team create more compelling content, but it also built stronger relationships with their ideal customers.

Improved collaboration. Through this process, Sophia's entire marketing team worked more closely together. Plus, the way the sales team, product managers, customer success, and marketing collaborated improved, too. Sales was more eager to work with marketing now that they'd aligned on their 3 Ps and messaging. The sales team saw how the content that their marketers created generated more leads and drove high-quality conversations with prospects. The startup's product managers also felt well-aligned with marketing and sales. They were especially clear on how marketing helped drive retention and an increase in customers completing "valuable actions." The team moved more quickly than ever, with tighter alignment and improved cross-functional communication.

"If I could do it all over again," Sophia said, "I would have nailed down our messaging in the earliest days of starting this company. I would have aligned my team right from the start. Messaging is part of everything we do to acquire and retain customers. Unfortunately, I let everyone figure out what to say on their own for too long, and it cost us."

Don't make these same mistakes. Now is the time to get *your* messaging and content strategy primed to accelerate growth.

Once you've reached this point, your entire team can move forward with confidence, knowing they have effective messaging and content for every phase of the marketing process. When the team uses your new product messages consistently, you'll increase customer acquisition and retention. Everyone will make more customer-centric decisions. You now have the keys to make your startup stand out. Cheers to your startup's growth ahead!

ABOUT THE AUTHOR

Allyson Letteri is a marketing executive who's spent her career building marketing teams at fast-growing tech companies in Silicon Valley (Intuit, Thumbtack, and Handshake). Now she advises founders and leaders at VC-backed startups so they can fast-track marketing decisions and build teams that deliver results. Allyson works with dozens of startups a year to help them to build their marketing strategy and achieve their growth goals.

Allyson started her career at Boston Consulting Group (BCG), focused on marketing and growth strategy projects. She especially loved her days in the field conducting customer and competitive research across the country for big-name brands. She then became a Product Marketer at Intuit, leading mobile payments and QuickBooks launches across the globe, from Singapore to Bangalore, Toronto to London.

At Thumbtack, Allyson built the Pro Marketing team and launched many new marketing strategies to attract and engage service professionals on the platform. She then moved to Handshake, where she was VP of Corporate and Student Marketing, leading a brand refresh and bringing millions of students onto the platform to get hired.

Through her experience building marketing teams from scratch to scale, Allyson knows how to create strong acquisition and retention engines for startups. In 2021, Allyson shifted her focus to advising early stage tech startup leaders on marketing strategy, positioning, content, and team design. Allyson also partners with leading venture capital firms to accelerate their portfolios' marketing success.

Allyson lives in San Francisco with her husband and two active kids. When she's not working with startup leaders, she's usually on adventures with her family and friends, painting with watercolors, or walking near the Golden Gate Bridge. She holds an MBA from the Stanford Graduate School of Business. She earned a BS in Business Administration and a BA in Political Science from the University of North Carolina at Chapel Hill, in her home state.

CONNECT WITH ALLYSON

Allyson works with startups in a range of ways, including:

✦ **Messaging sprints.** Allyson will guide your team through each step in this book so you can develop your 3 Ps, strong messaging, and high-converting content.

✦ **1:1 advising.** Allyson advises startup founders and leaders on a wide range of marketing topics, helping them launch effective marketing strategies and build engaged teams.

✦ **Workshops.** Allyson designs and facilitates workshops for individual startups and VC's portfolios to help startups develop their go-to-market strategies and accelerate growth.

Contact Allyson Letteri
allysonletteri.com
hello@allysonletteri.com

STANDOUT STARTUP TOOLKIT

DOWNLOAD THE TOOLKIT

This book is filled with step-by-step guidance and useful templates so you can create an effective messaging and content strategy. Download a free toolkit with the templates and worksheets from *Standout Startup*, ready for you to complete. It's the fastest way to take action and get results.

allysonletteri.com/toolkit

REVIEW THE BOOK

Thank you for reading *Standout Startup*! I hope you've found it valuable, and I'd love for you to share your feedback. Please leave a review. This will help other startup leaders find and benefit from this book, too.

Made in United States
Orlando, FL
29 December 2023

41808311R00157